D0923155

SUPERHEROES ON A MEDICAL MISSION

"... WITH BILL?"
MEDIKIDZ EXPLAIN EPILEPSY

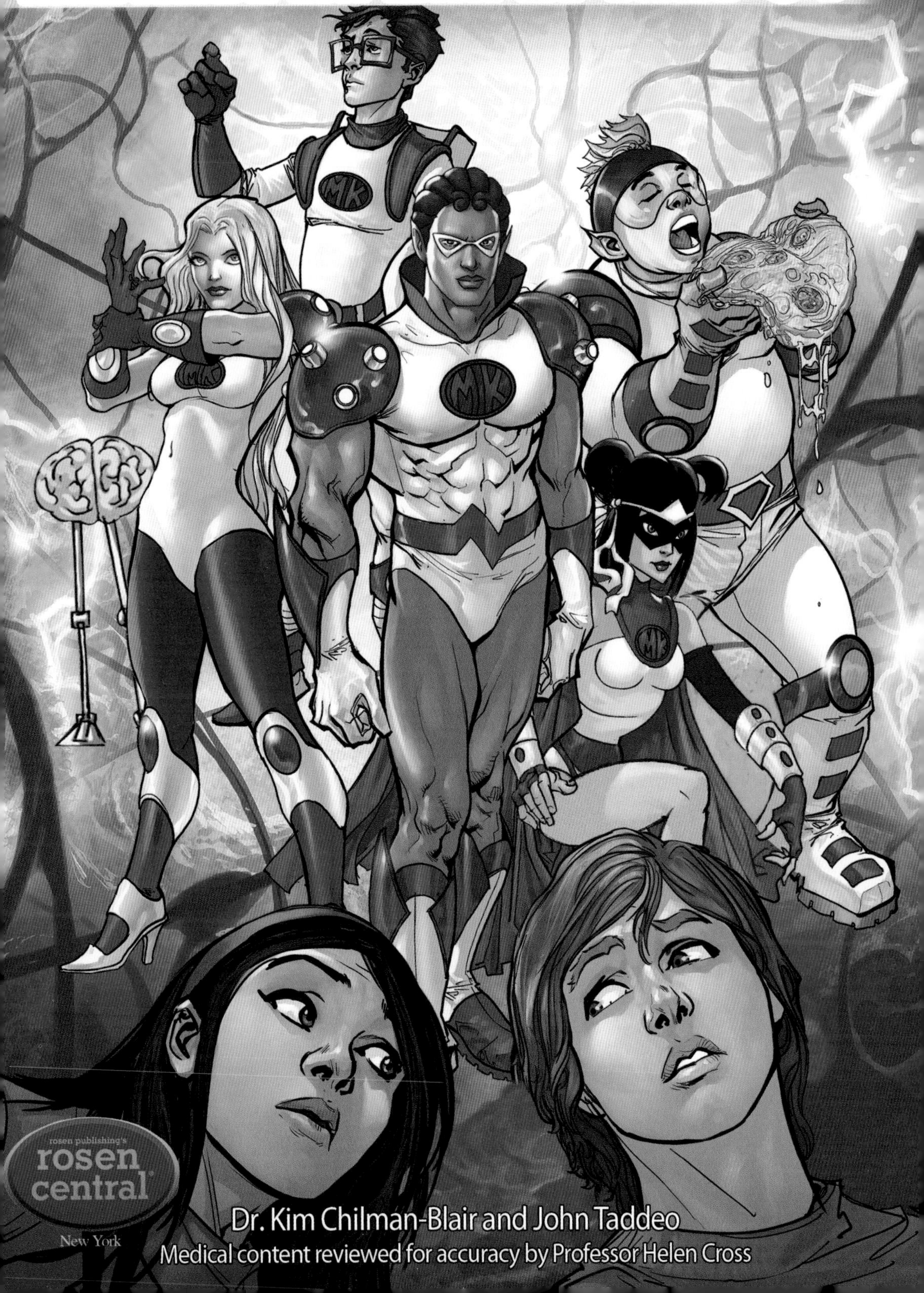

rosen publishing's
rosen central
New York

Dr. Kim Chilman-Blair and John Taddeo
Medical content reviewed for accuracy by Professor Helen Cross

This edition published in 2010 by:

The Rosen Publishing Group, Inc.
29 East 21st Street
New York, NY 10010

Additional end matter copyright © 2010 by The Rosen Publishing Group, Inc.

Library of Congress Cataloging-in-Publication Data

Chilman-Blair, Kim.
"What's up with Bill?": medikidz explain epilepsy / Dr. Kim Chilman-Blair and John Taddeo; medical content reviewed for accuracy by Professor Helen Cross.
    p. cm.—(Superheroes on a medical mission)
Includes index.
ISBN 978-1-4358-3533-7 (library binding)
1. Epilepsy—Comic books, strips, etc. I. Taddeo, John. II. Title.
RC372.2.C45 2010
616.8'53—dc22

2009029785

Manufactured in China

CPSIA Compliance Information: Batch #MW0102YA: For Further Information contact Rosen Publishing, New York, New York at 1-800-237-9932

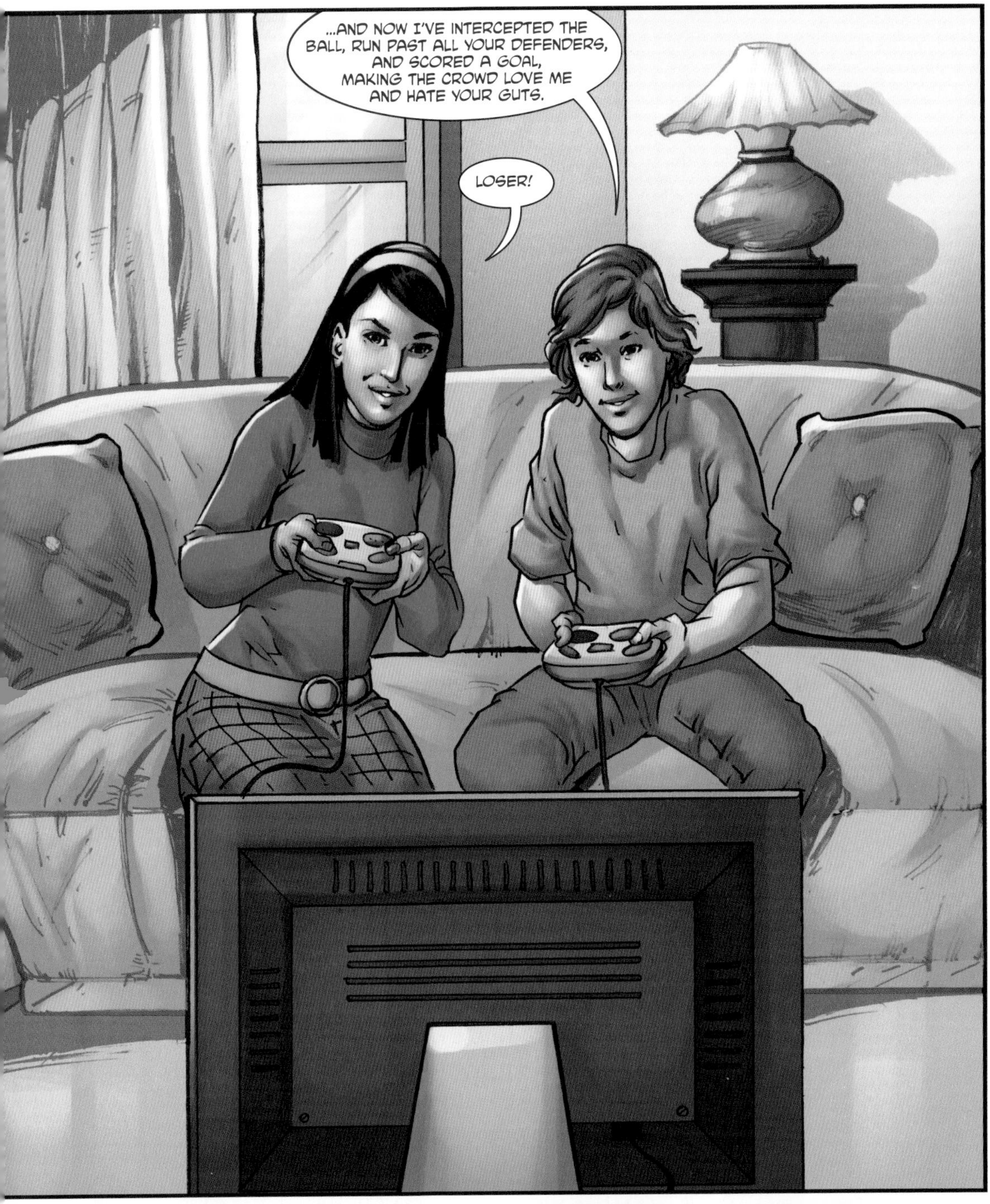
...AND NOW I'VE INTERCEPTED THE BALL, RUN PAST ALL YOUR DEFENDERS, AND SCORED A GOAL, MAKING THE CROWD LOVE ME AND HATE YOUR GUTS.
LOSER!

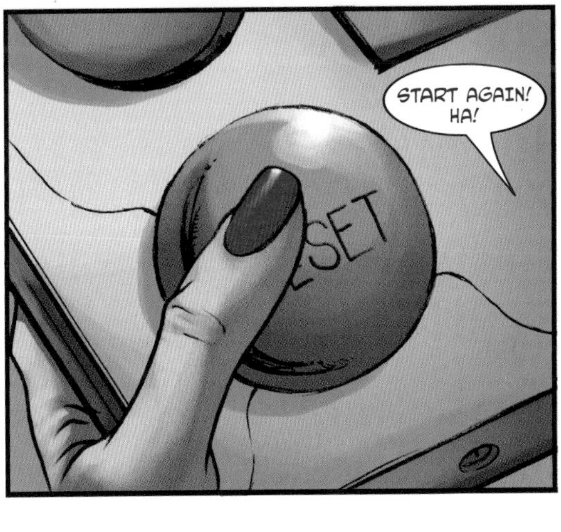
START AGAIN! HA!
SET

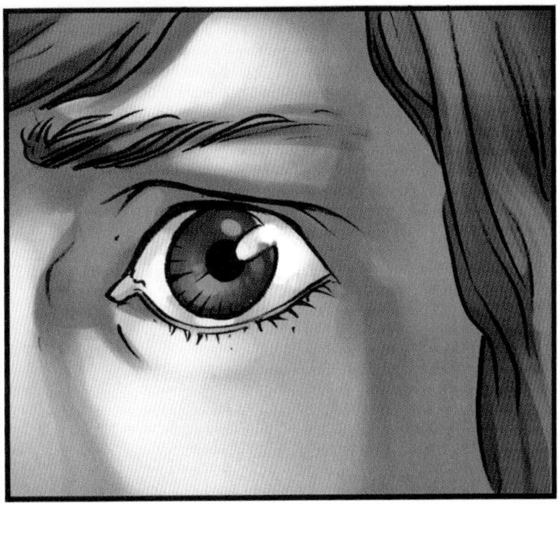

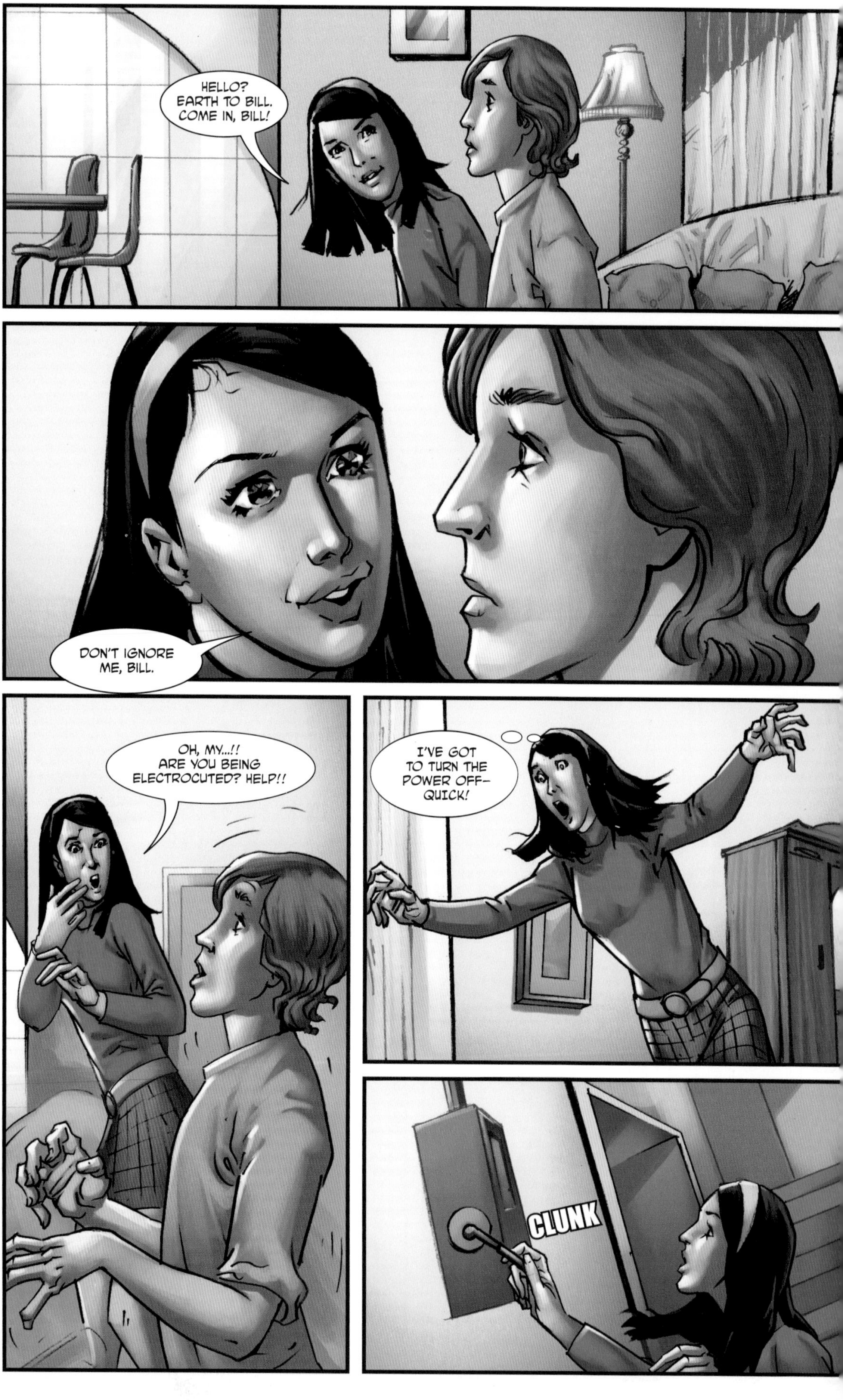
HELLO? EARTH TO BILL. COME IN, BILL!
DON'T IGNORE ME, BILL.
OH, MY...!! ARE YOU BEING ELECTROCUTED? HELP!!
I'VE GOT TO TURN THE POWER OFF– QUICK!
CLUNK

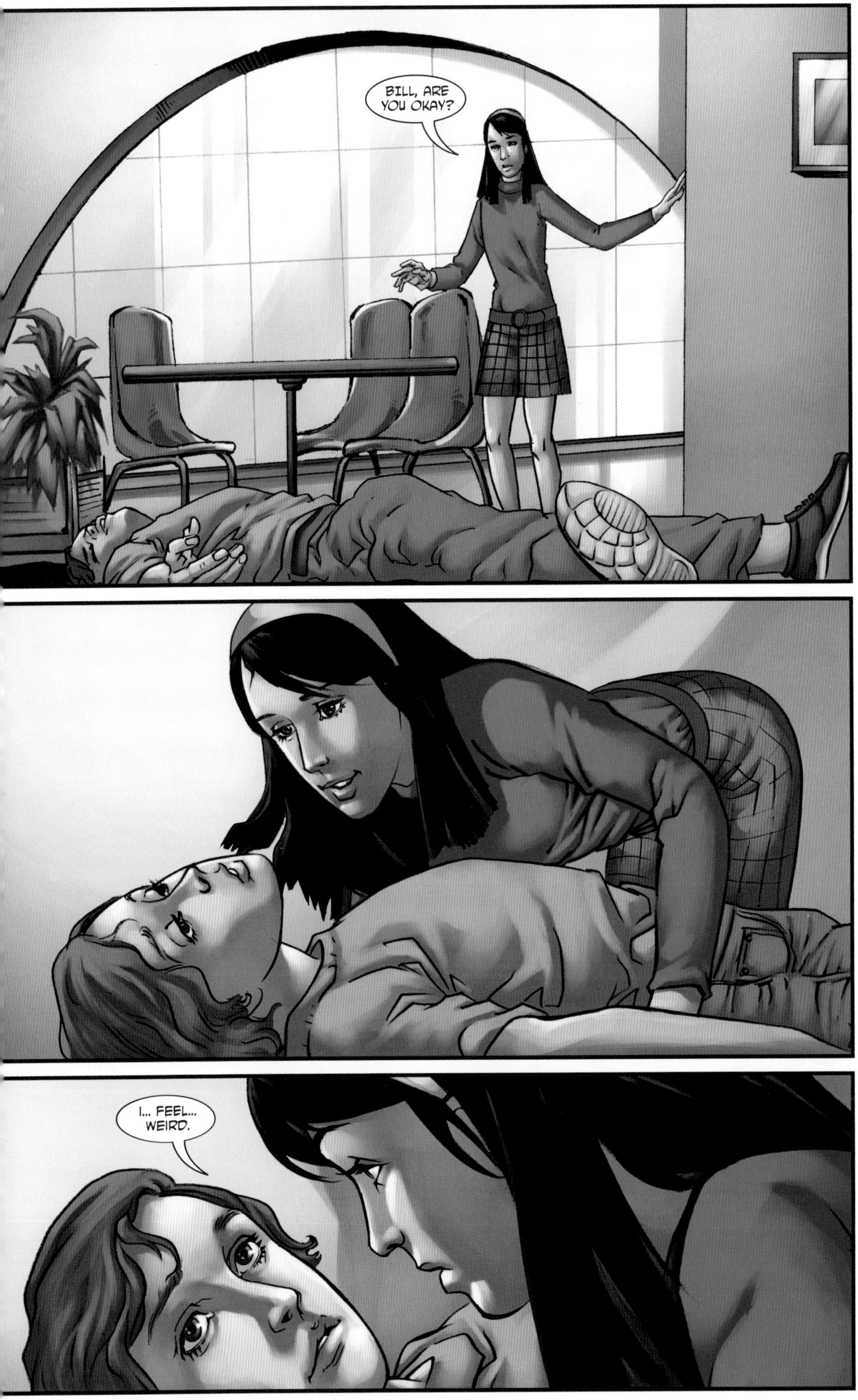
BILL, ARE YOU OKAY?
I... FEEL... WEIRD.

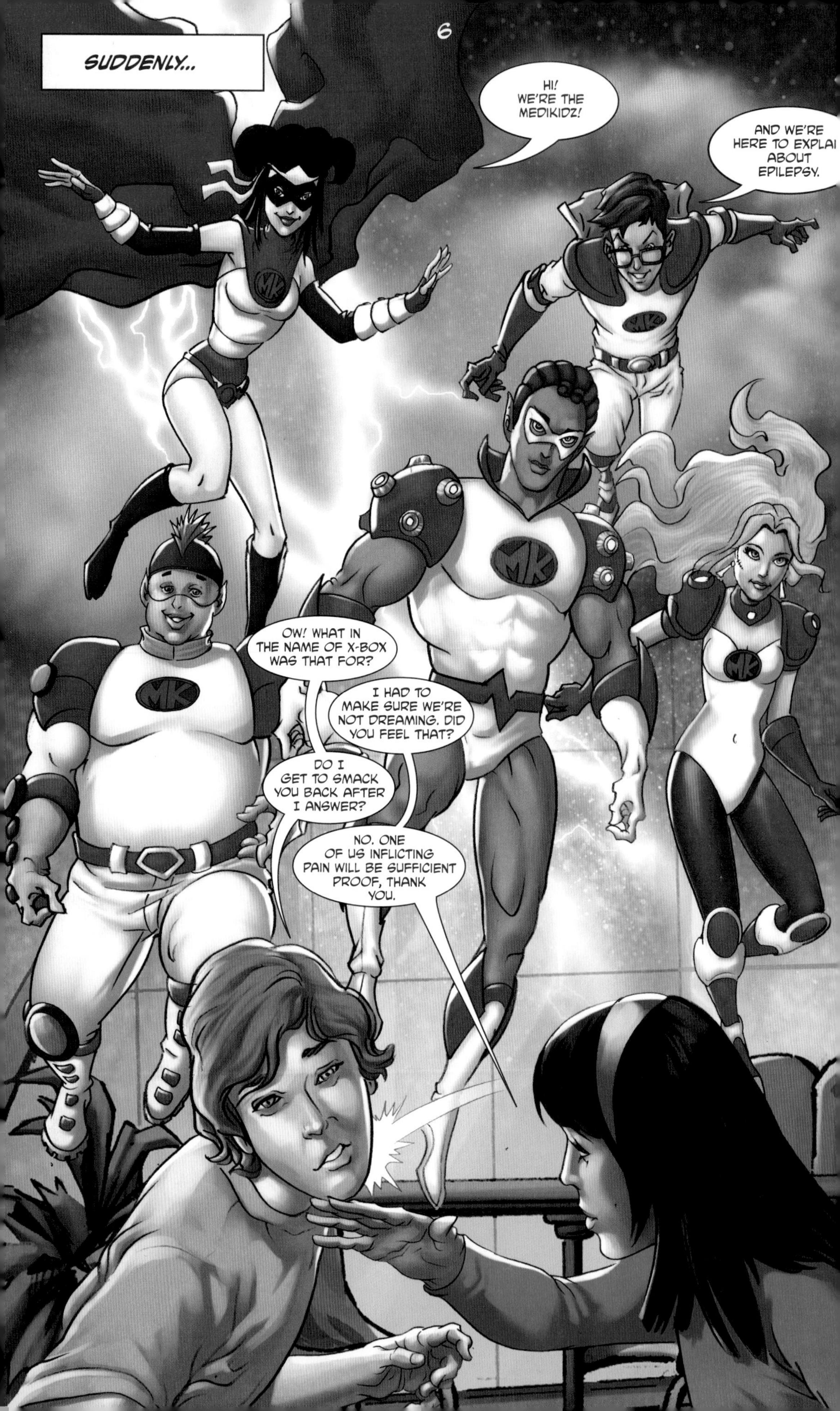
6
SUDDENLY...
HI! WE'RE THE MEDIKIDZ!
AND WE'RE HERE TO EXPLAI ABOUT EPILEPSY.
OW! WHAT IN THE NAME OF X-BOX WAS THAT FOR?
I HAD TO MAKE SURE WE'RE NOT DREAMING. DID YOU FEEL THAT?
DO I GET TO SMACK YOU BACK AFTER I ANSWER?
NO. ONE OF US INFLICTING PAIN WILL BE SUFFICIENT PROOF, THANK YOU.

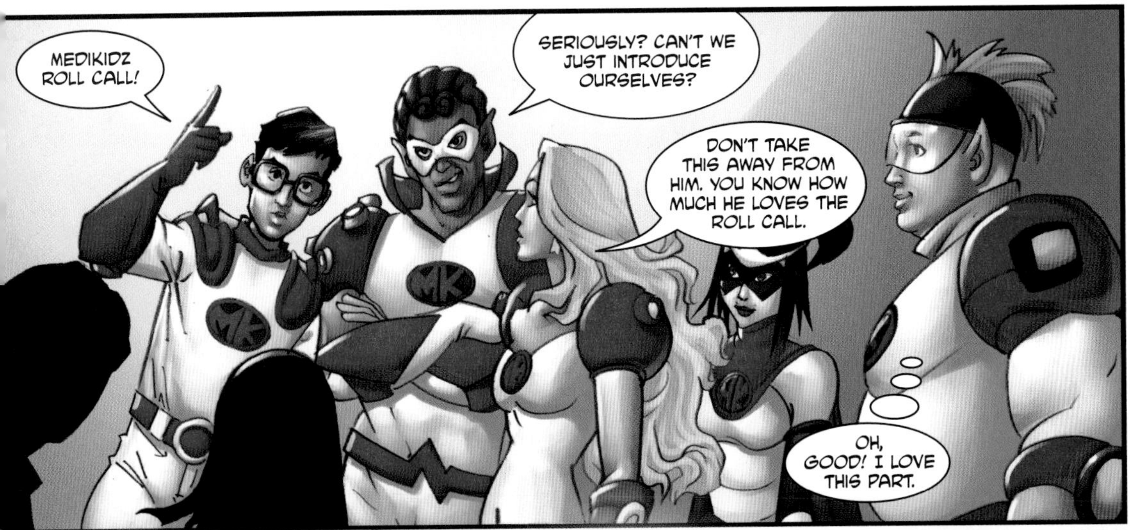
MEDIKIDZ ROLL CALL!
SERIOUSLY? CAN'T WE JUST INTRODUCE OURSELVES?
DON'T TAKE THIS AWAY FROM HIM. YOU KNOW HOW MUCH HE LOVES THE ROLL CALL.
OH, GOOD! I LOVE THIS PART.

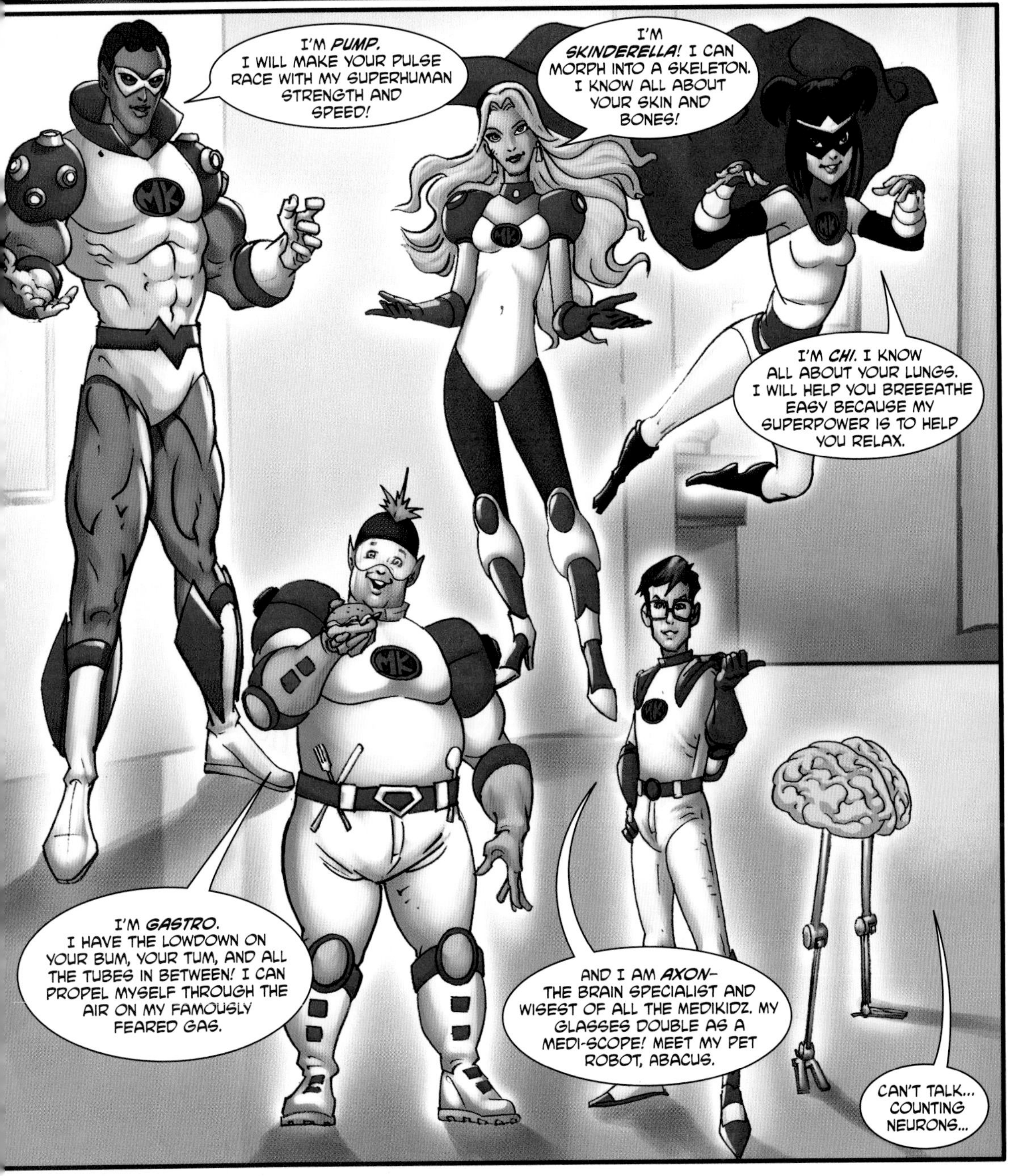
I'M *PUMP*. I WILL MAKE YOUR PULSE RACE WITH MY SUPERHUMAN STRENGTH AND SPEED!
I'M *SKINDERELLA*! I CAN MORPH INTO A SKELETON. I KNOW ALL ABOUT YOUR SKIN AND BONES!
I'M *CHI*. I KNOW ALL ABOUT YOUR LUNGS. I WILL HELP YOU BREEEATHE EASY BECAUSE MY SUPERPOWER IS TO HELP YOU RELAX.
I'M *GASTRO*. I HAVE THE LOWDOWN ON YOUR BUM, YOUR TUM, AND ALL THE TUBES IN BETWEEN! I CAN PROPEL MYSELF THROUGH THE AIR ON MY FAMOUSLY FEARED GAS.
AND I AM *AXON*– THE BRAIN SPECIALIST AND WISEST OF ALL THE MEDIKIDZ. MY GLASSES DOUBLE AS A MEDI-SCOPE! MEET MY PET ROBOT, ABACUS.
CAN'T TALK... COUNTING NEURONS...

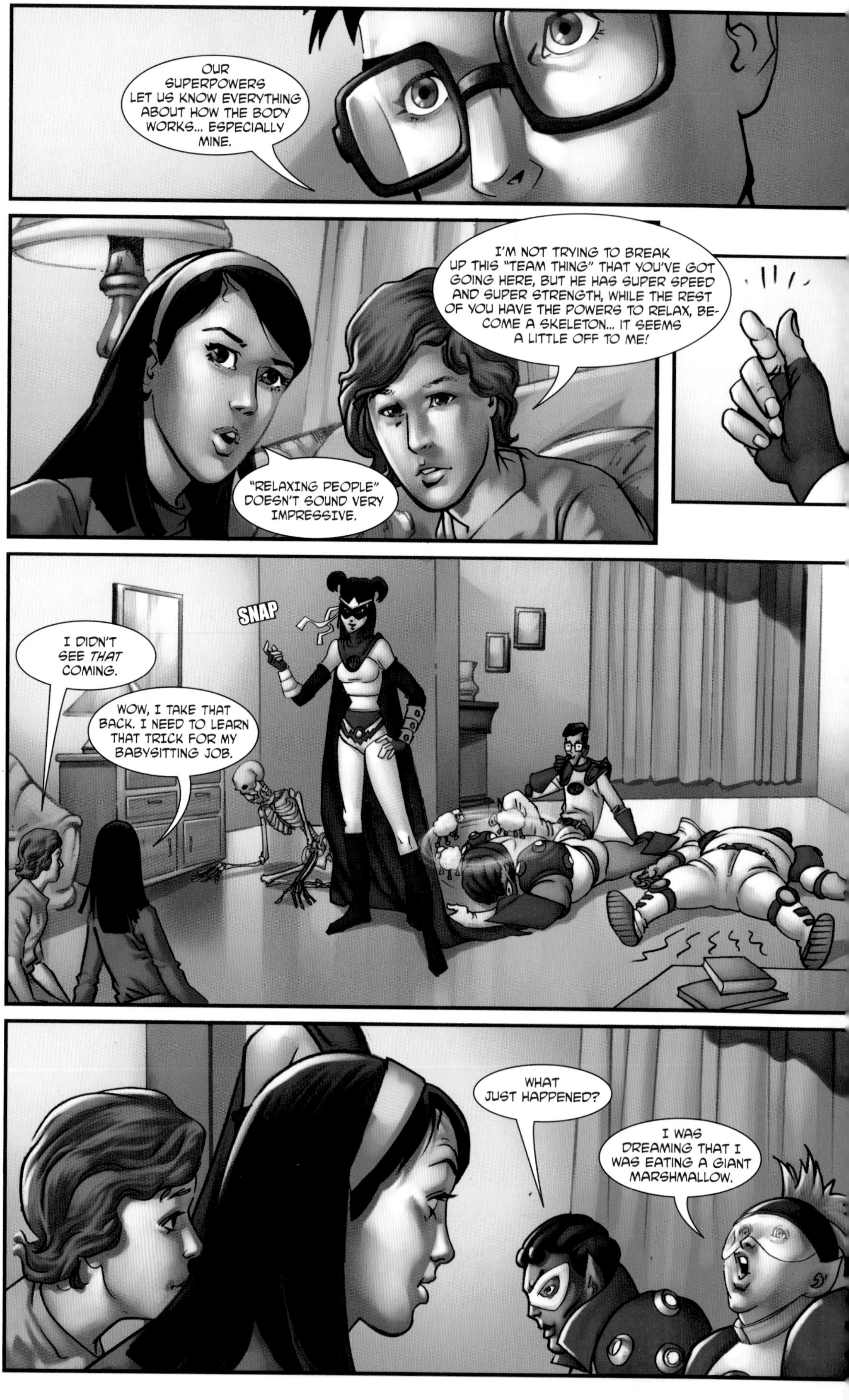
OUR SUPERPOWERS LET US KNOW EVERYTHING ABOUT HOW THE BODY WORKS... ESPECIALLY MINE.
I'M NOT TRYING TO BREAK UP THIS "TEAM THING" THAT YOU'VE GOT GOING HERE, BUT HE HAS SUPER SPEED AND SUPER STRENGTH, WHILE THE REST OF YOU HAVE THE POWERS TO RELAX, BE-COME A SKELETON... IT SEEMS A LITTLE OFF TO ME!
"RELAXING PEOPLE" DOESN'T SOUND VERY IMPRESSIVE.
SNAP
I DIDN'T SEE *THAT* COMING.
WOW, I TAKE THAT BACK. I NEED TO LEARN THAT TRICK FOR MY BABYSITTING JOB.
WHAT JUST HAPPENED?
I WAS DREAMING THAT I WAS EATING A GIANT MARSHMALLOW.

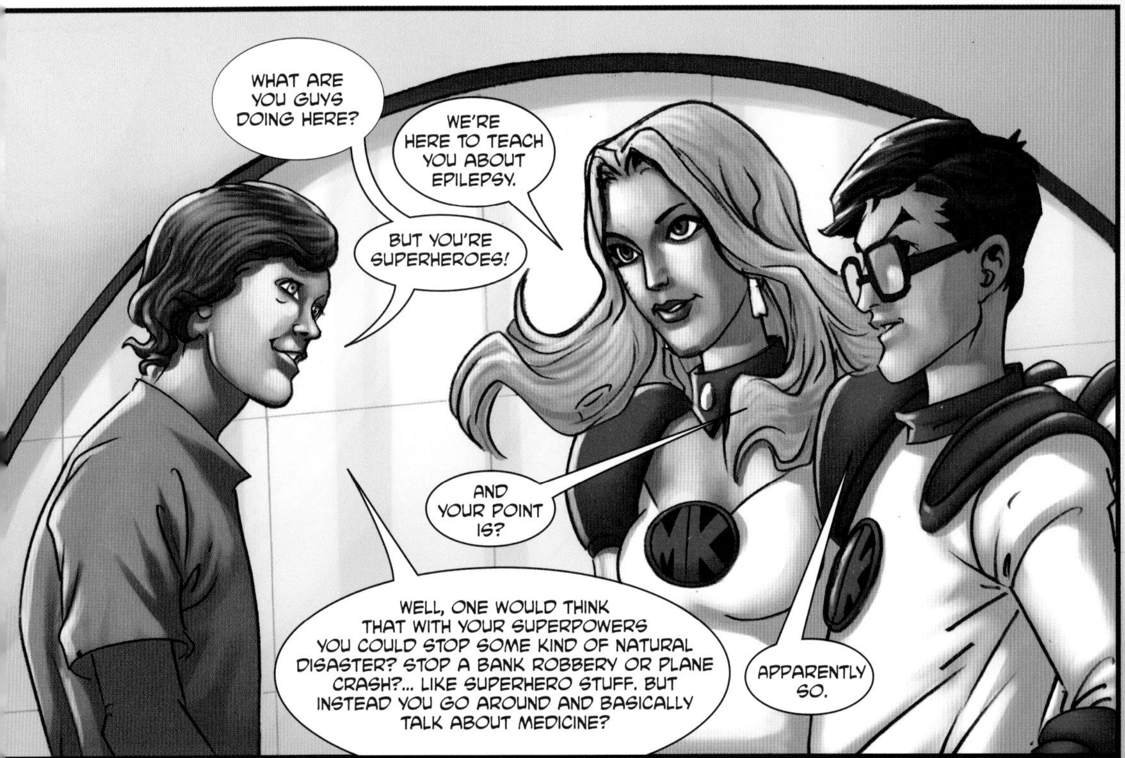
WHAT ARE YOU GUYS DOING HERE?
WE'RE HERE TO TEACH YOU ABOUT EPILEPSY.
BUT YOU'RE SUPERHEROES!
AND YOUR POINT IS?
WELL, ONE WOULD THINK THAT WITH YOUR SUPERPOWERS YOU COULD STOP SOME KIND OF NATURAL DISASTER? STOP A BANK ROBBERY OR PLANE CRASH?... LIKE SUPERHERO STUFF. BUT INSTEAD YOU GO AROUND AND BASICALLY TALK ABOUT MEDICINE?
APPARENTLY SO.

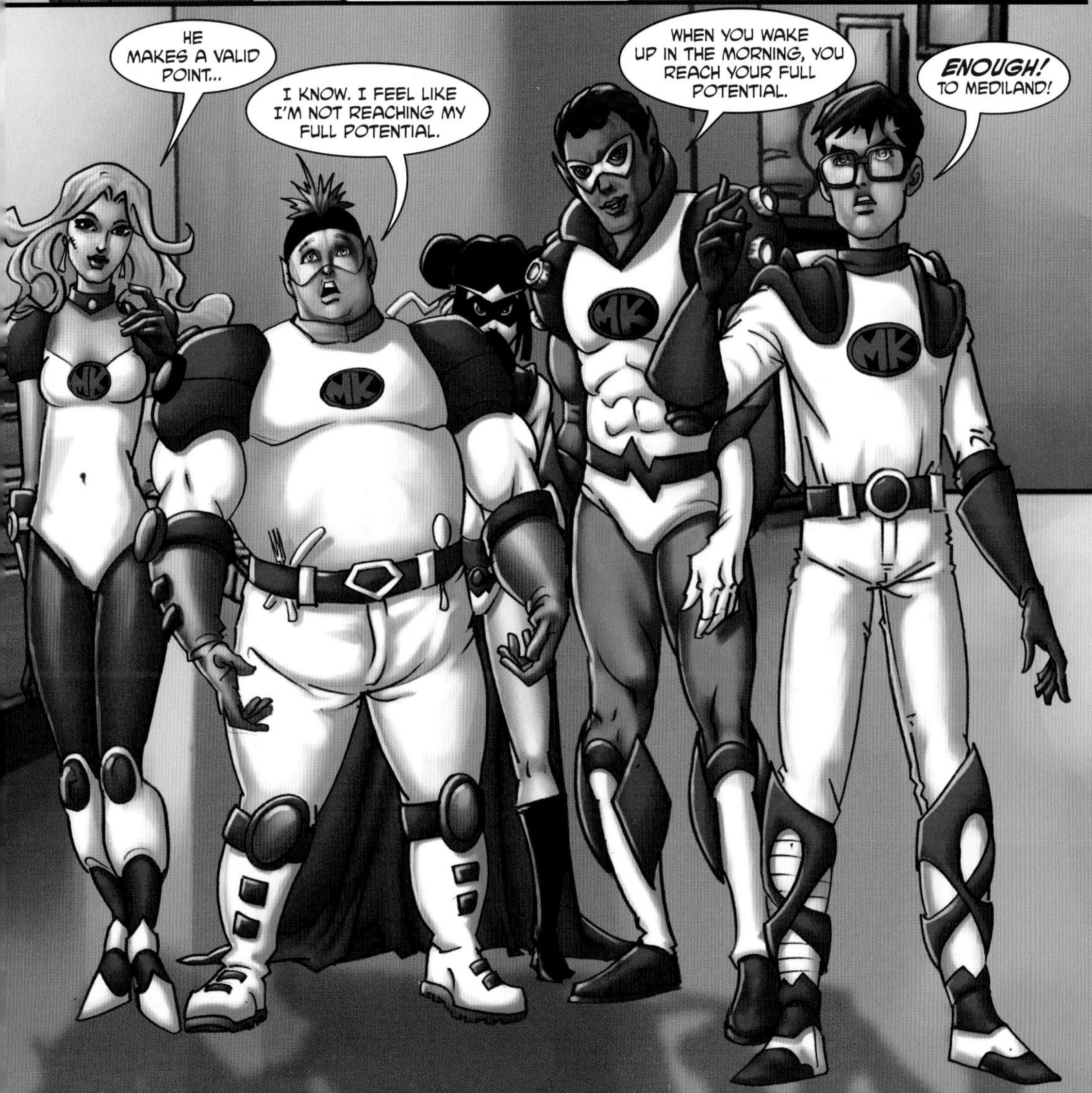
HE MAKES A VALID POINT...
I KNOW. I FEEL LIKE I'M NOT REACHING MY FULL POTENTIAL.
WHEN YOU WAKE UP IN THE MORNING, YOU REACH YOUR FULL POTENTIAL.
ENOUGH! TO MEDILAND!

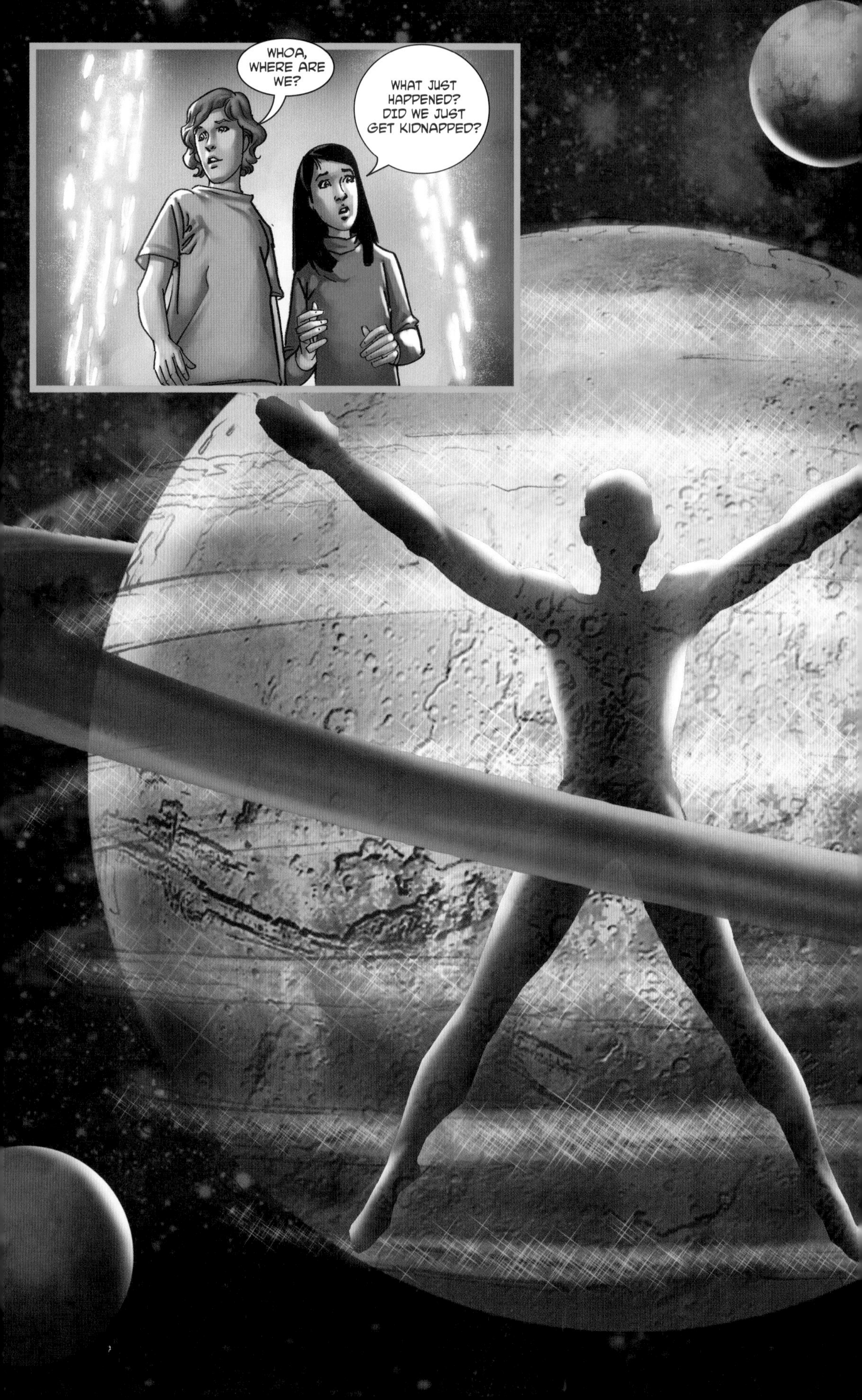
WHOA, WHERE ARE WE?
WHAT JUST HAPPENED? DID WE JUST GET KIDNAPPED?

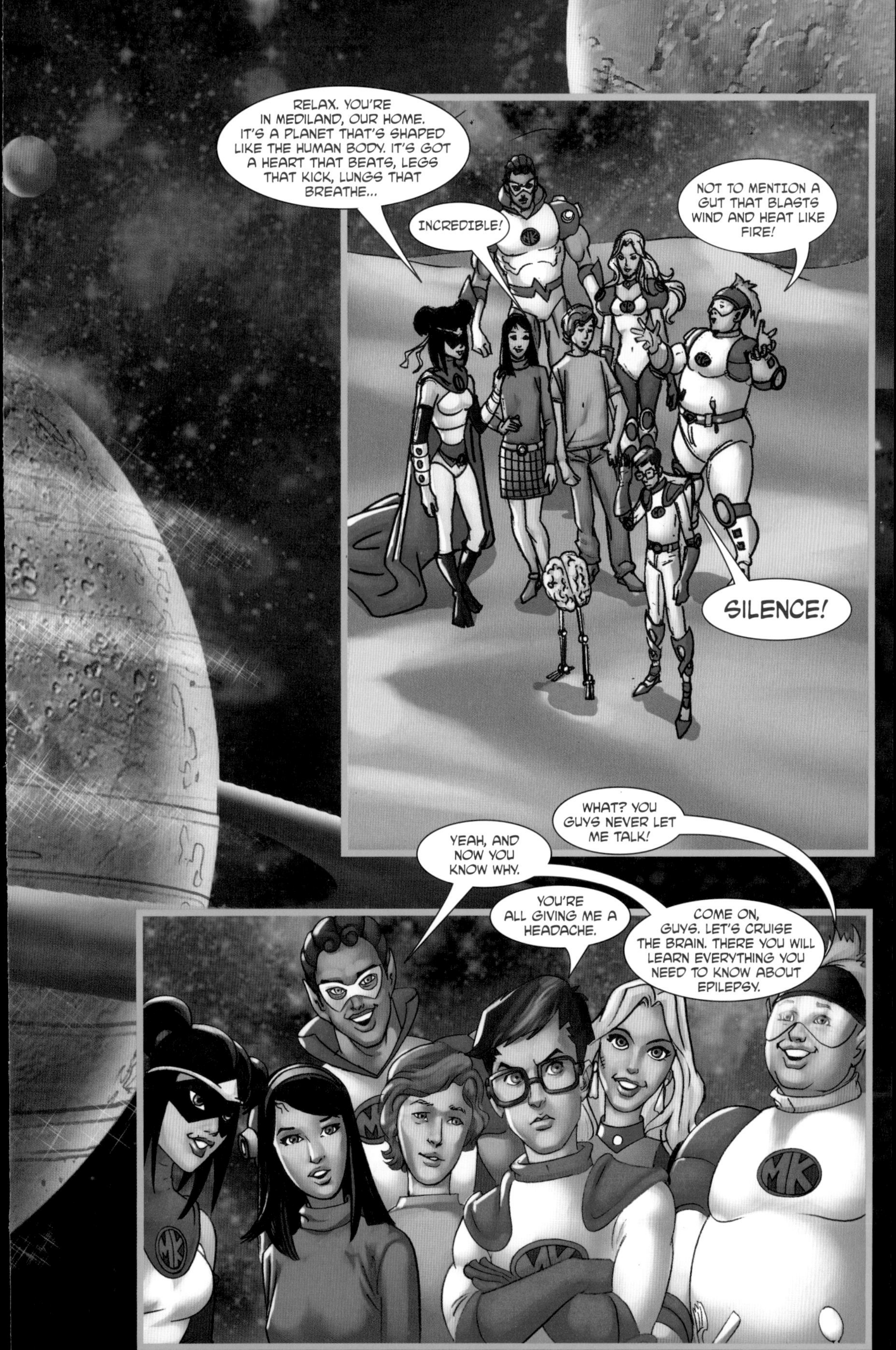
RELAX. YOU'RE IN MEDILAND, OUR HOME. IT'S A PLANET THAT'S SHAPED LIKE THE HUMAN BODY. IT'S GOT A HEART THAT BEATS, LEGS THAT KICK, LUNGS THAT BREATHE...
INCREDIBLE!
NOT TO MENTION A GUT THAT BLASTS WIND AND HEAT LIKE FIRE!
SILENCE!
WHAT? YOU GUYS NEVER LET ME TALK!
YEAH, AND NOW YOU KNOW WHY.
YOU'RE ALL GIVING ME A HEADACHE.
COME ON, GUYS. LET'S CRUISE THE BRAIN. THERE YOU WILL LEARN EVERYTHING YOU NEED TO KNOW ABOUT EPILEPSY.

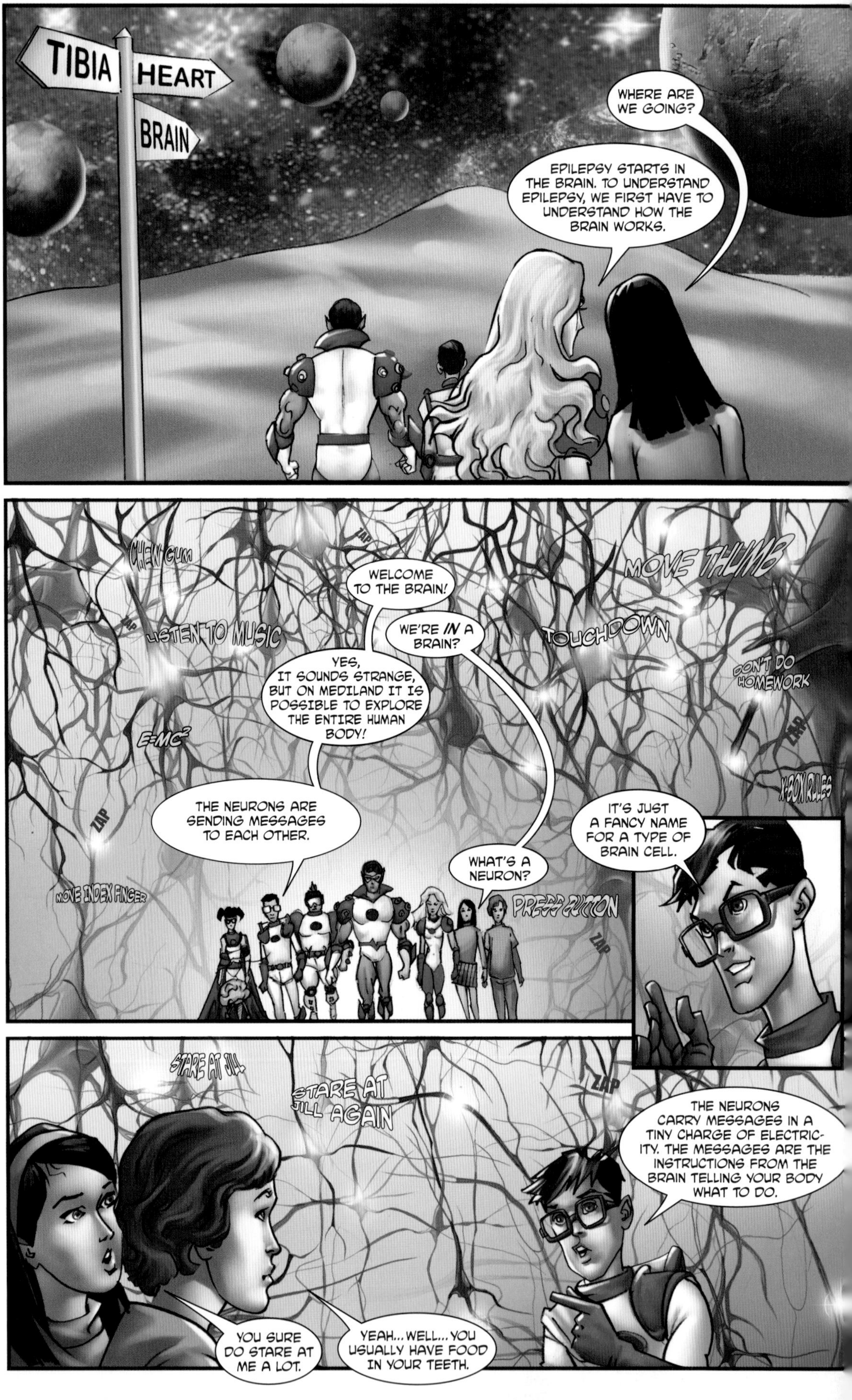
TIBIA
HEART
BRAIN
WHERE ARE WE GOING?
EPILEPSY STARTS IN THE BRAIN. TO UNDERSTAND EPILEPSY, WE FIRST HAVE TO UNDERSTAND HOW THE BRAIN WORKS.
CHEW GUM
ZAP
LISTEN TO MUSIC
MOVE THUMB
TOUCHDOWN
DON'T DO HOMEWORK
E=MC2
X-BOX RULES
MOVE INDEX FINGER
PRESS BUTTON
WELCOME TO THE BRAIN!
WE'RE *IN* A BRAIN?
YES, IT SOUNDS STRANGE, BUT ON MEDILAND IT IS POSSIBLE TO EXPLORE THE ENTIRE HUMAN BODY!
THE NEURONS ARE SENDING MESSAGES TO EACH OTHER.
WHAT'S A NEURON?
IT'S JUST A FANCY NAME FOR A TYPE OF BRAIN CELL.
STARE AT JILL
STARE AT JILL AGAIN
ZAP
THE NEURONS CARRY MESSAGES IN A TINY CHARGE OF ELECTRIC-ITY. THE MESSAGES ARE THE INSTRUCTIONS FROM THE BRAIN TELLING YOUR BODY WHAT TO DO.
YOU SURE DO STARE AT ME A LOT.
YEAH... WELL... YOU USUALLY HAVE FOOD IN YOUR TEETH.

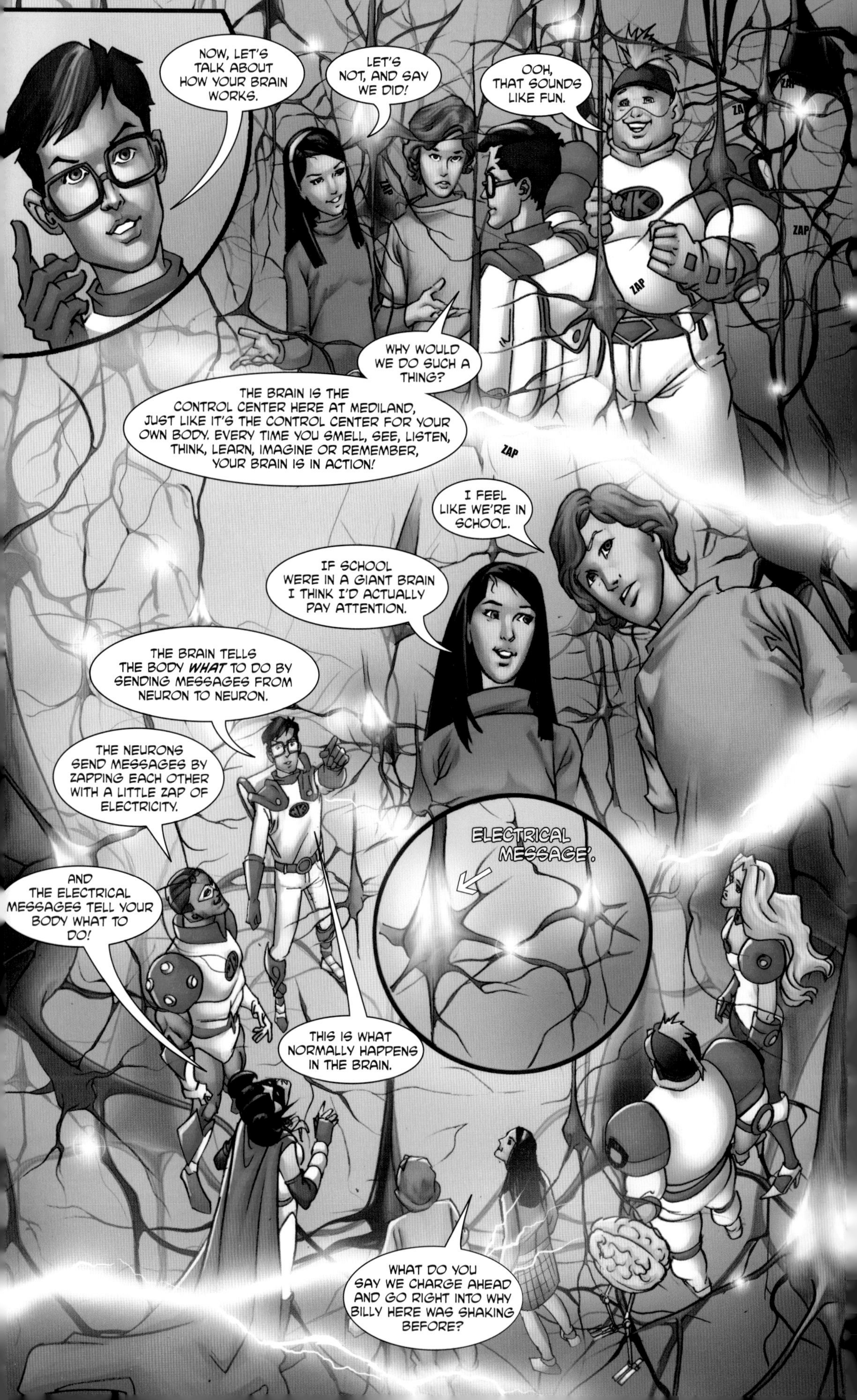
NOW, LET'S TALK ABOUT HOW YOUR BRAIN WORKS.
LET'S NOT, AND SAY WE DID!
OOH, THAT SOUNDS LIKE FUN.
ZAP
ZAP
ZAP
ZAP
WHY WOULD WE DO SUCH A THING?
THE BRAIN IS THE CONTROL CENTER HERE AT MEDILAND, JUST LIKE IT'S THE CONTROL CENTER FOR YOUR OWN BODY. EVERY TIME YOU SMELL, SEE, LISTEN, THINK, LEARN, IMAGINE OR REMEMBER, YOUR BRAIN IS IN ACTION!
ZAP
I FEEL LIKE WE'RE IN SCHOOL.
IF SCHOOL WERE IN A GIANT BRAIN I THINK I'D ACTUALLY PAY ATTENTION.
THE BRAIN TELLS THE BODY ***WHAT*** TO DO BY SENDING MESSAGES FROM NEURON TO NEURON.
THE NEURONS SEND MESSAGES BY ZAPPING EACH OTHER WITH A LITTLE ZAP OF ELECTRICITY.
ELECTRICAL MESSAGE.
AND THE ELECTRICAL MESSAGES TELL YOUR BODY WHAT TO DO!
THIS IS WHAT NORMALLY HAPPENS IN THE BRAIN.
WHAT DO YOU SAY WE CHARGE AHEAD AND GO RIGHT INTO WHY BILLY HERE WAS SHAKING BEFORE?

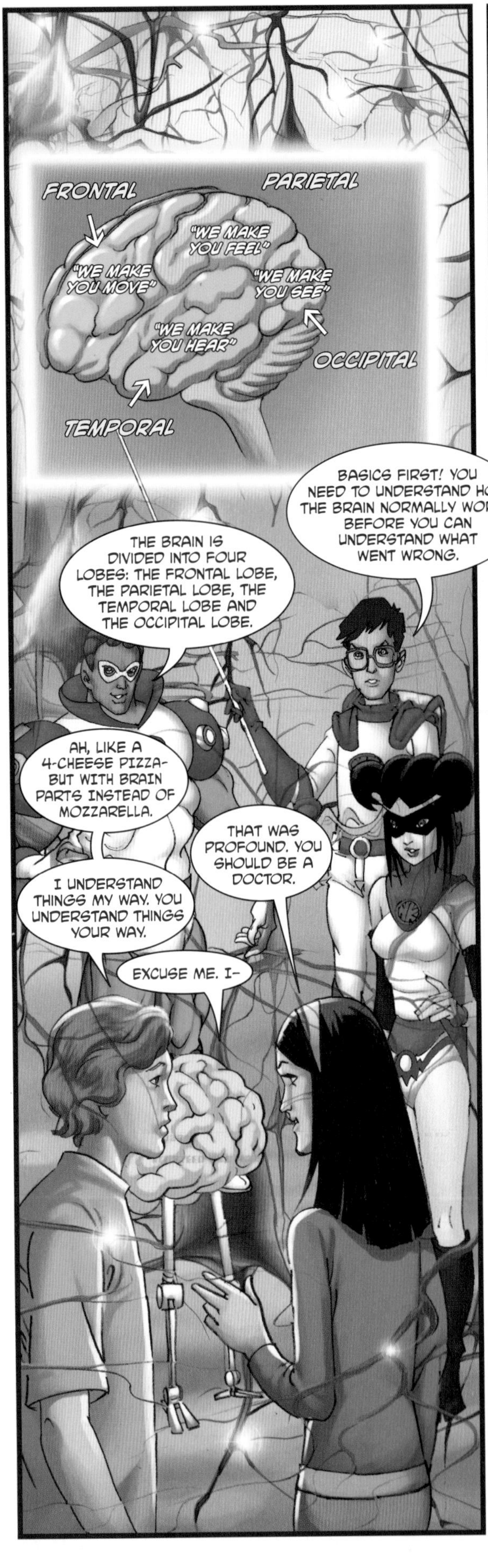
FRONTAL
PARIETAL
"WE MAKE YOU FEEL"
"WE MAKE YOU MOVE"
"WE MAKE YOU SEE"
"WE MAKE YOU HEAR"
OCCIPITAL
TEMPORAL
BASICS FIRST! YOU NEED TO UNDERSTAND HOW THE BRAIN NORMALLY WORKS BEFORE YOU CAN UNDERSTAND WHAT WENT WRONG.
THE BRAIN IS DIVIDED INTO FOUR LOBES: THE FRONTAL LOBE, THE PARIETAL LOBE, THE TEMPORAL LOBE AND THE OCCIPITAL LOBE.
AH, LIKE A 4-CHEESE PIZZA- BUT WITH BRAIN PARTS INSTEAD OF MOZZARELLA.
THAT WAS PROFOUND. YOU SHOULD BE A DOCTOR.
I UNDERSTAND THINGS MY WAY. YOU UNDERSTAND THINGS YOUR WAY.
EXCUSE ME. I-

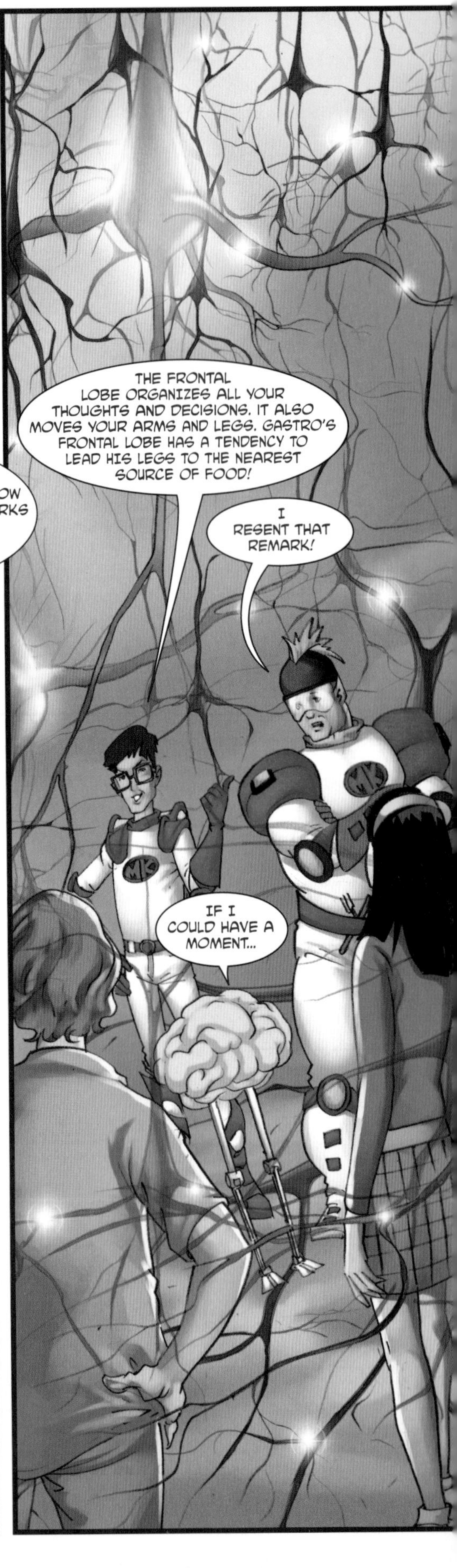
THE FRONTAL LOBE ORGANIZES ALL YOUR THOUGHTS AND DECISIONS. IT ALSO MOVES YOUR ARMS AND LEGS. GASTRO'S FRONTAL LOBE HAS A TENDENCY TO LEAD HIS LEGS TO THE NEAREST SOURCE OF FOOD!
I RESENT THAT REMARK!
IF I COULD HAVE A MOMENT...

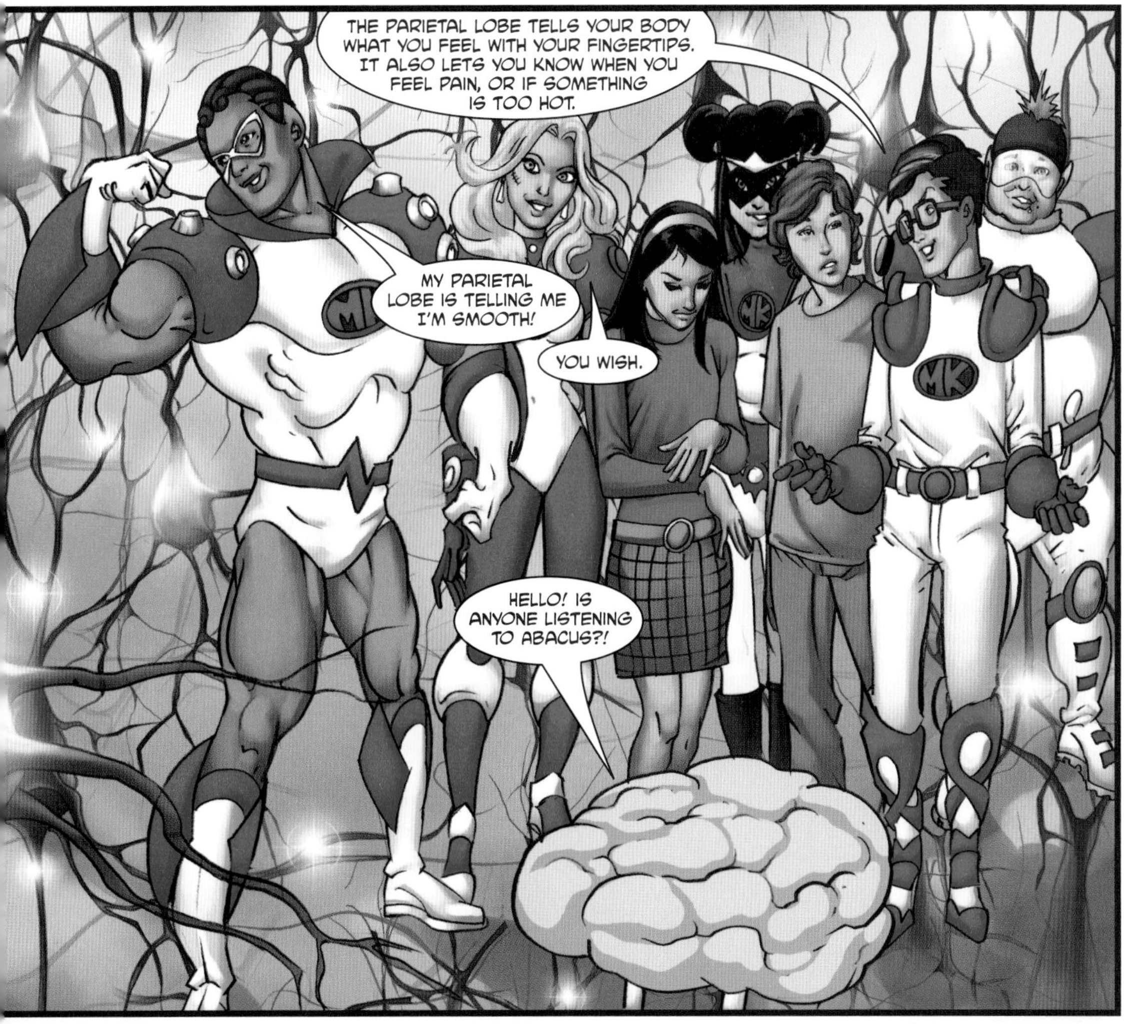
THE PARIETAL LOBE TELLS YOUR BODY WHAT YOU FEEL WITH YOUR FINGERTIPS. IT ALSO LETS YOU KNOW WHEN YOU FEEL PAIN, OR IF SOMETHING IS TOO HOT.
MY PARIETAL LOBE IS TELLING ME I'M SMOOTH!
YOU WISH.
HELLO! IS ANYONE LISTENING TO ABACUS?!

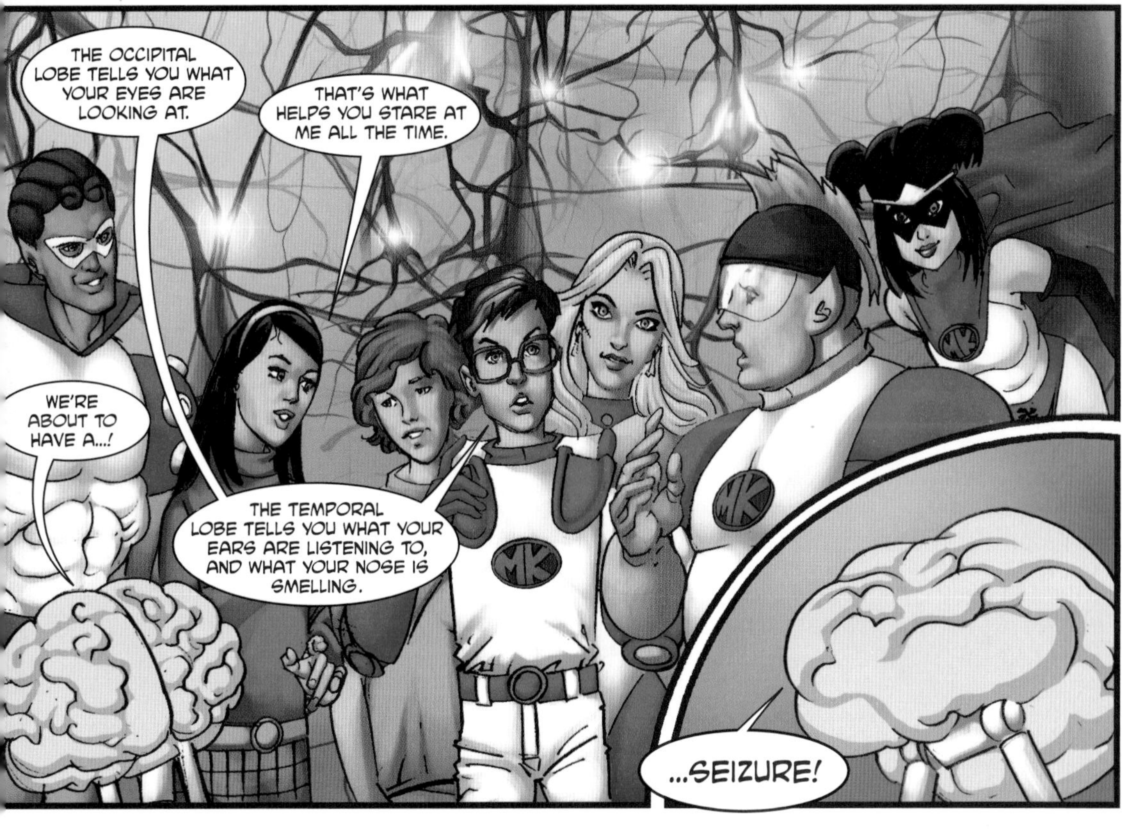
THE OCCIPITAL LOBE TELLS YOU WHAT YOUR EYES ARE LOOKING AT.
THAT'S WHAT HELPS YOU STARE AT ME ALL THE TIME.
WE'RE ABOUT TO HAVE A...!
THE TEMPORAL LOBE TELLS YOU WHAT YOUR EARS ARE LISTENING TO, AND WHAT YOUR NOSE IS SMELLING.
...SEIZURE!

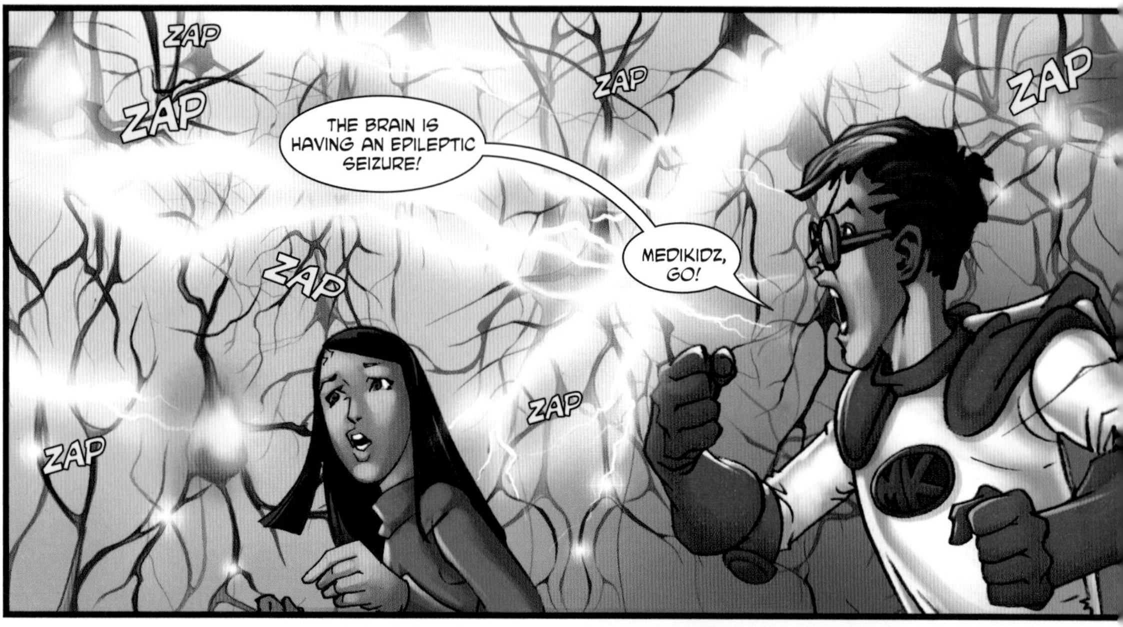
ZAP
ZAP
ZAP
ZAP
THE BRAIN IS HAVING AN EPILEPTIC SEIZURE!
MEDIKIDZ, GO!
ZAP
ZAP
ZAP

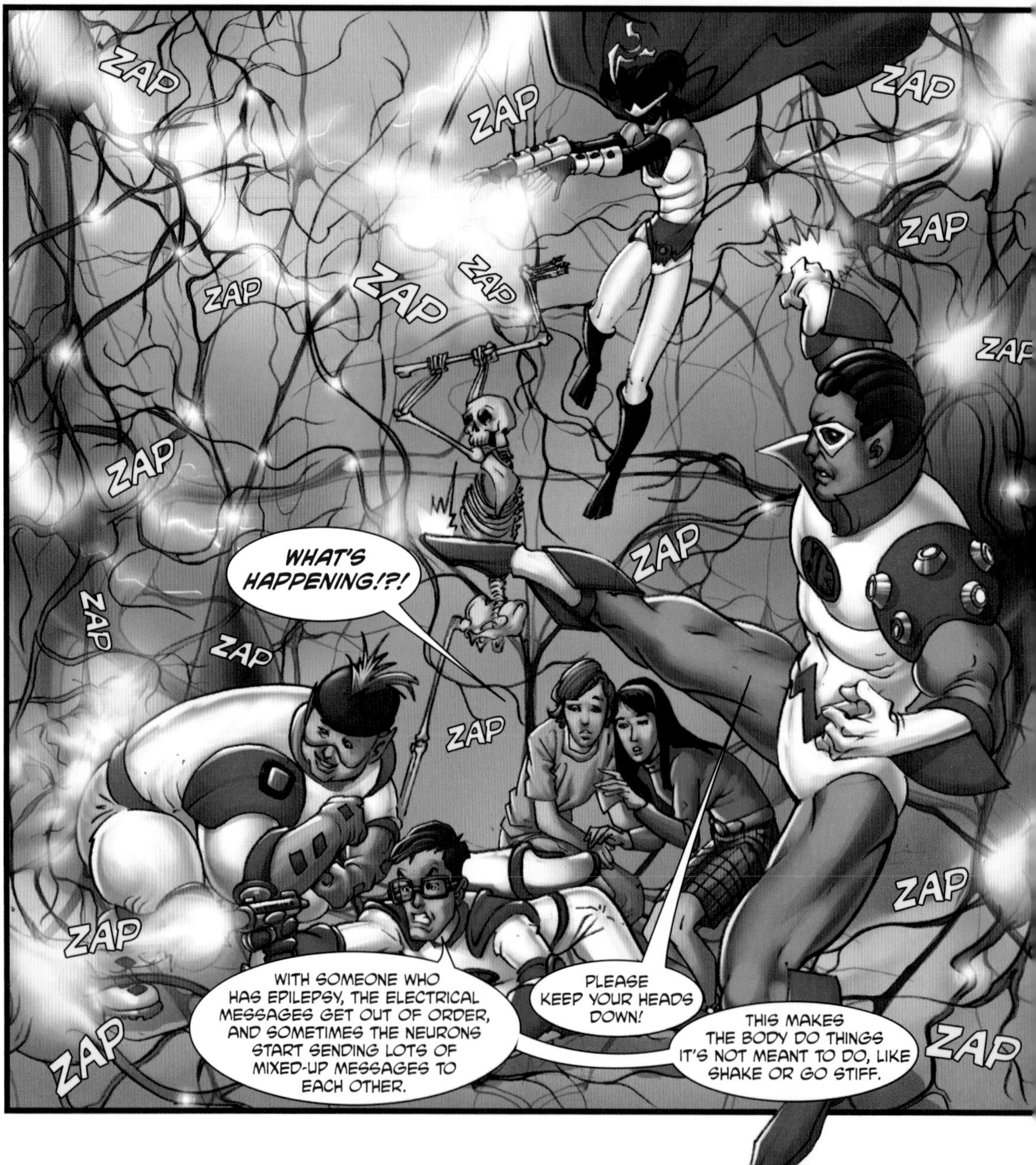
ZAP
ZAP
ZAP
ZAP
ZAP
ZAP
ZAP
ZAP
ZAP
WHAT'S HAPPENING!?!
ZAP
ZAP
ZAP
ZAP
ZAP
WITH SOMEONE WHO HAS EPILEPSY, THE ELECTRICAL MESSAGES GET OUT OF ORDER, AND SOMETIMES THE NEURONS START SENDING LOTS OF MIXED-UP MESSAGES TO EACH OTHER.
PLEASE KEEP YOUR HEADS DOWN!
THIS MAKES THE BODY DO THINGS IT'S NOT MEANT TO DO, LIKE SHAKE OR GO STIFF.
ZAP
ZAP

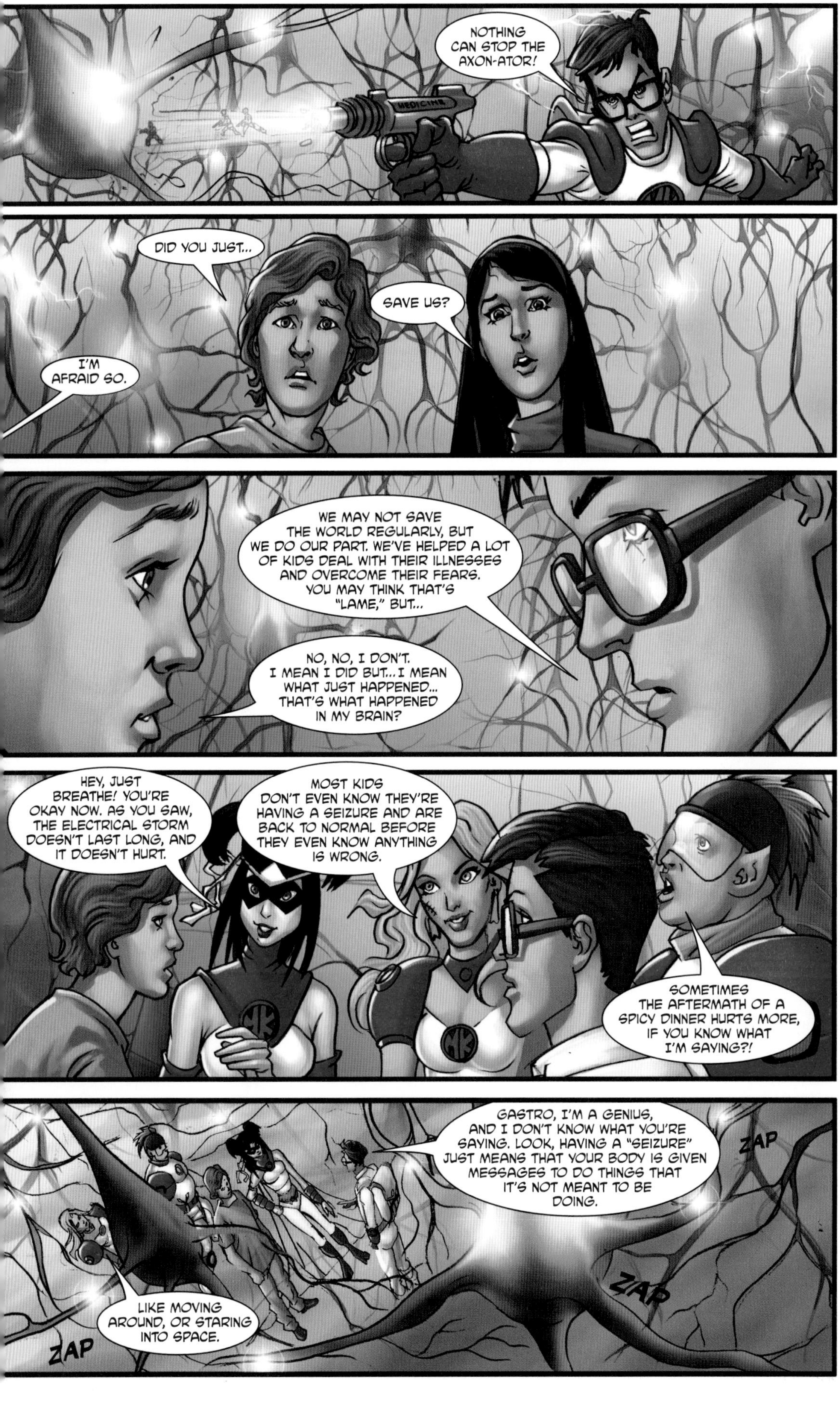
NOTHING CAN STOP THE AXON-ATOR!
MEDICINE
DID YOU JUST...
SAVE US?
I'M AFRAID SO.
WE MAY NOT SAVE THE WORLD REGULARLY, BUT WE DO OUR PART. WE'VE HELPED A LOT OF KIDS DEAL WITH THEIR ILLNESSES AND OVERCOME THEIR FEARS. YOU MAY THINK THAT'S "LAME," BUT...
NO, NO, I DON'T. I MEAN I DID BUT... I MEAN WHAT JUST HAPPENED... THAT'S WHAT HAPPENED IN MY BRAIN?
HEY, JUST BREATHE! YOU'RE OKAY NOW. AS YOU SAW, THE ELECTRICAL STORM DOESN'T LAST LONG, AND IT DOESN'T HURT.
MOST KIDS DON'T EVEN KNOW THEY'RE HAVING A SEIZURE AND ARE BACK TO NORMAL BEFORE THEY EVEN KNOW ANYTHING IS WRONG.
SOMETIMES THE AFTERMATH OF A SPICY DINNER HURTS MORE, IF YOU KNOW WHAT I'M SAYING?!
GASTRO, I'M A GENIUS, AND I DON'T KNOW WHAT YOU'RE SAYING. LOOK, HAVING A "SEIZURE" JUST MEANS THAT YOUR BODY IS GIVEN MESSAGES TO DO THINGS THAT IT'S NOT MEANT TO BE DOING.
LIKE MOVING AROUND, OR STARING INTO SPACE.
ZAP
ZAP
ZAP

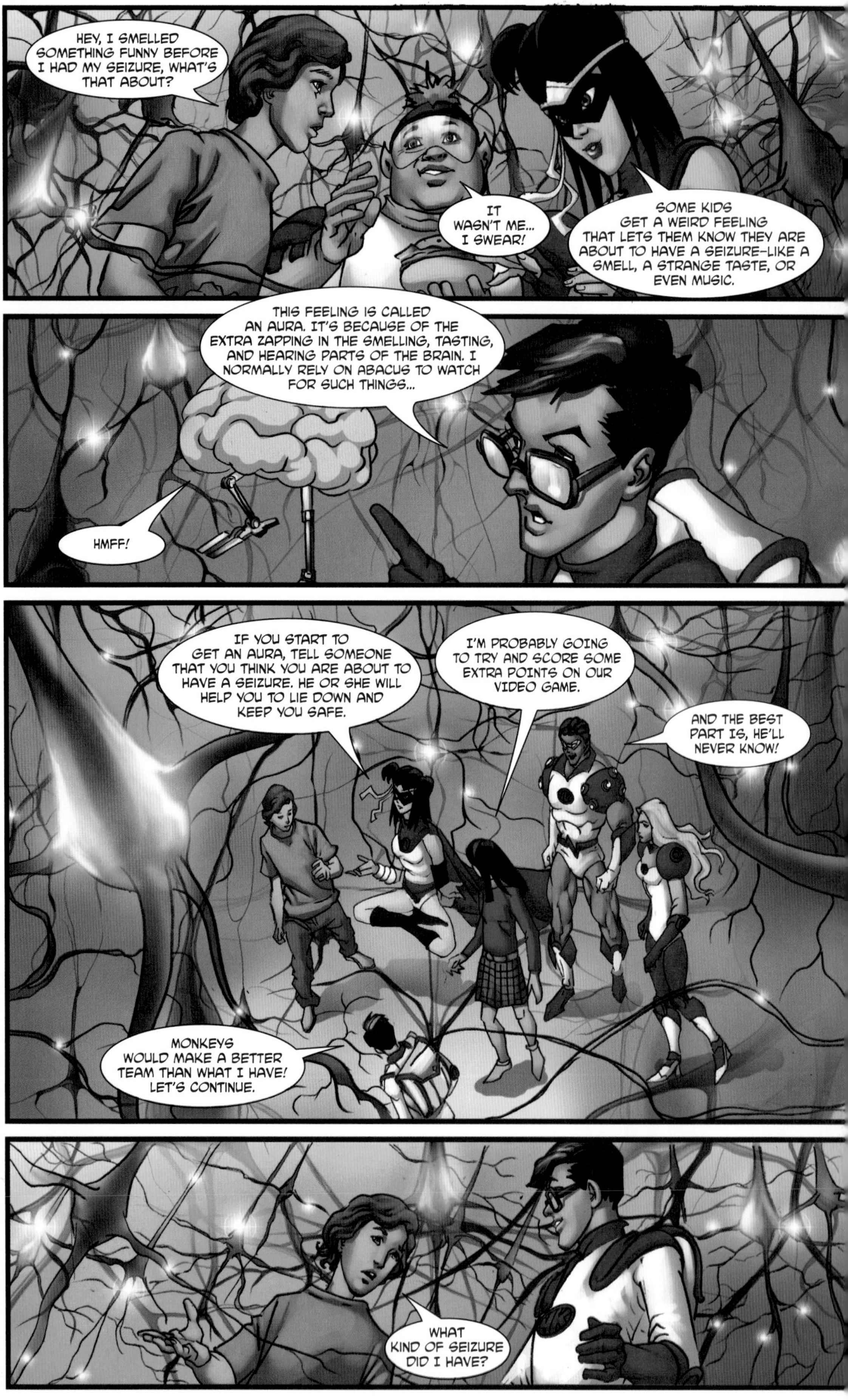
HEY, I SMELLED SOMETHING FUNNY BEFORE I HAD MY SEIZURE, WHAT'S THAT ABOUT?
IT WASN'T ME... I SWEAR!
SOME KIDS GET A WEIRD FEELING THAT LETS THEM KNOW THEY ARE ABOUT TO HAVE A SEIZURE–LIKE A SMELL, A STRANGE TASTE, OR EVEN MUSIC.
THIS FEELING IS CALLED AN AURA. IT'S BECAUSE OF THE EXTRA ZAPPING IN THE SMELLING, TASTING, AND HEARING PARTS OF THE BRAIN. I NORMALLY RELY ON ABACUS TO WATCH FOR SUCH THINGS...
HMFF!
IF YOU START TO GET AN AURA, TELL SOMEONE THAT YOU THINK YOU ARE ABOUT TO HAVE A SEIZURE. HE OR SHE WILL HELP YOU TO LIE DOWN AND KEEP YOU SAFE.
I'M PROBABLY GOING TO TRY AND SCORE SOME EXTRA POINTS ON OUR VIDEO GAME.
AND THE BEST PART IS, HE'LL NEVER KNOW!
MONKEYS WOULD MAKE A BETTER TEAM THAN WHAT I HAVE! LET'S CONTINUE.
WHAT KIND OF SEIZURE DID I HAVE?

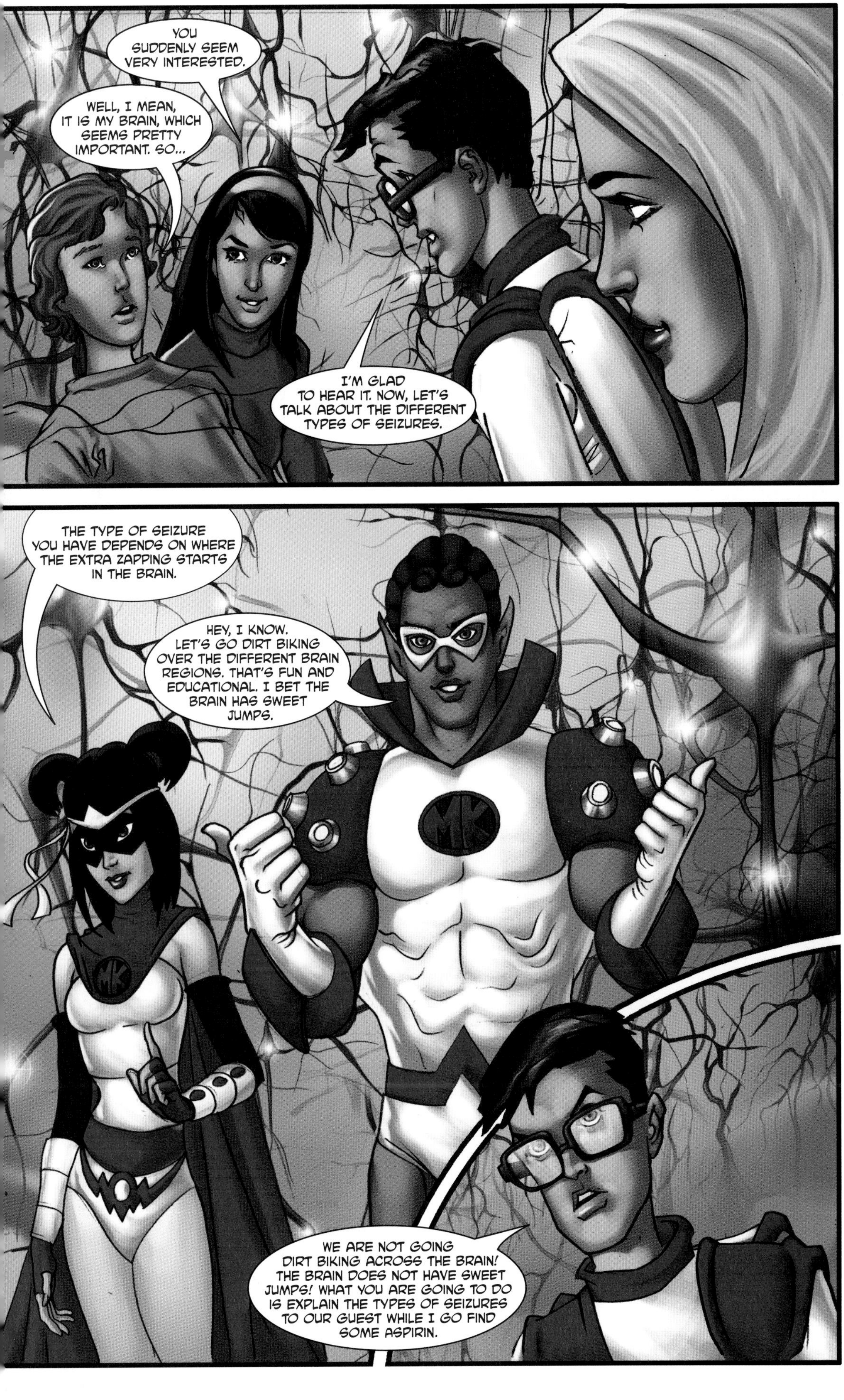
YOU SUDDENLY SEEM VERY INTERESTED.
WELL, I MEAN, IT IS MY BRAIN, WHICH SEEMS PRETTY IMPORTANT. SO...
I'M GLAD TO HEAR IT. NOW, LET'S TALK ABOUT THE DIFFERENT TYPES OF SEIZURES.
THE TYPE OF SEIZURE YOU HAVE DEPENDS ON WHERE THE EXTRA ZAPPING STARTS IN THE BRAIN.
HEY, I KNOW. LET'S GO DIRT BIKING OVER THE DIFFERENT BRAIN REGIONS. THAT'S FUN AND EDUCATIONAL. I BET THE BRAIN HAS SWEET JUMPS.
WE ARE NOT GOING DIRT BIKING ACROSS THE BRAIN! THE BRAIN DOES NOT HAVE SWEET JUMPS! WHAT YOU ARE GOING TO DO IS EXPLAIN THE TYPES OF SEIZURES TO OUR GUEST WHILE I GO FIND SOME ASPIRIN.

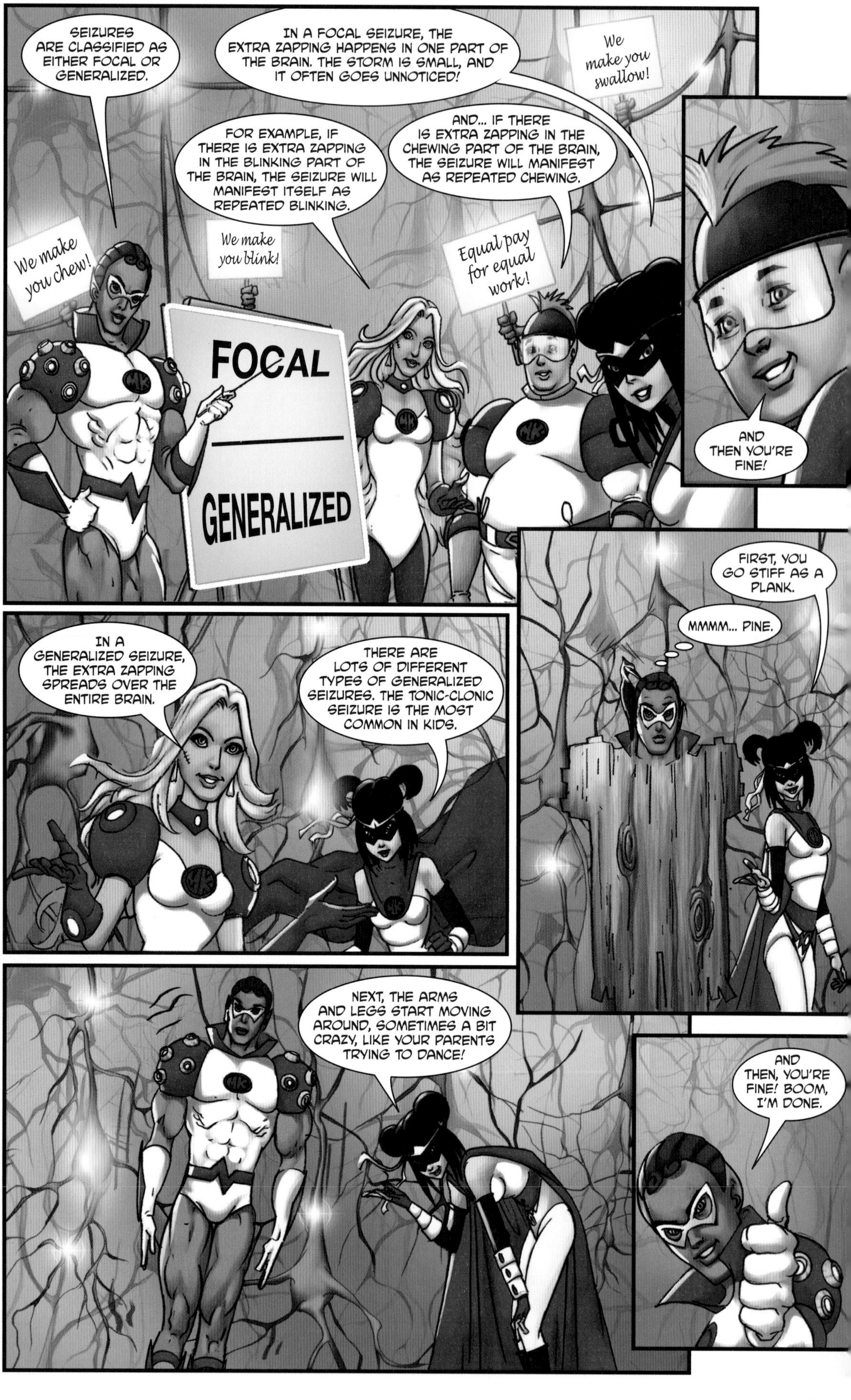
SEIZURES ARE CLASSIFIED AS EITHER FOCAL OR GENERALIZED.
IN A FOCAL SEIZURE, THE EXTRA ZAPPING HAPPENS IN ONE PART OF THE BRAIN. THE STORM IS SMALL, AND IT OFTEN GOES UNNOTICED!
We make you swallow!
FOR EXAMPLE, IF THERE IS EXTRA ZAPPING IN THE BLINKING PART OF THE BRAIN, THE SEIZURE WILL MANIFEST ITSELF AS REPEATED BLINKING.
AND... IF THERE IS EXTRA ZAPPING IN THE CHEWING PART OF THE BRAIN, THE SEIZURE WILL MANIFEST AS REPEATED CHEWING.
We make you chew!
We make you blink!
Equal pay for equal work!
FOCAL
GENERALIZED
AND THEN YOU'RE FINE!
IN A GENERALIZED SEIZURE, THE EXTRA ZAPPING SPREADS OVER THE ENTIRE BRAIN.
THERE ARE LOTS OF DIFFERENT TYPES OF GENERALIZED SEIZURES. THE TONIC-CLONIC SEIZURE IS THE MOST COMMON IN KIDS.
FIRST, YOU GO STIFF AS A PLANK.
MMMM... PINE.
NEXT, THE ARMS AND LEGS START MOVING AROUND, SOMETIMES A BIT CRAZY, LIKE YOUR PARENTS TRYING TO DANCE!
AND THEN, YOU'RE FINE! BOOM, I'M DONE.

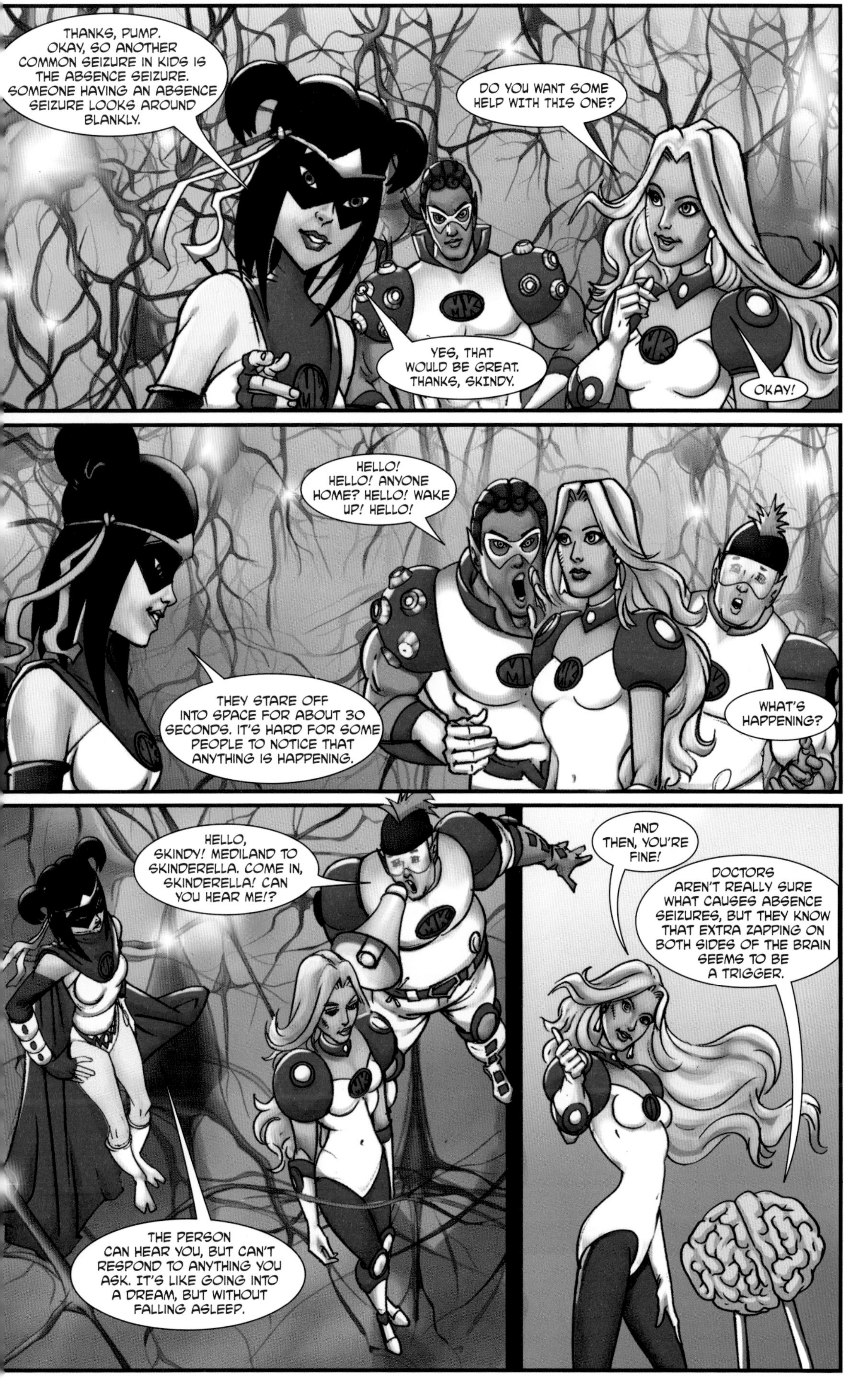
THANKS, PUMP. OKAY, SO ANOTHER COMMON SEIZURE IN KIDS IS THE ABSENCE SEIZURE. SOMEONE HAVING AN ABSENCE SEIZURE LOOKS AROUND BLANKLY.
DO YOU WANT SOME HELP WITH THIS ONE?
YES, THAT WOULD BE GREAT. THANKS, SKINDY.
OKAY!
HELLO! HELLO! ANYONE HOME? HELLO! WAKE UP! HELLO!
THEY STARE OFF INTO SPACE FOR ABOUT 30 SECONDS. IT'S HARD FOR SOME PEOPLE TO NOTICE THAT ANYTHING IS HAPPENING.
WHAT'S HAPPENING?
HELLO, SKINDY! MEDILAND TO SKINDERELLA. COME IN, SKINDERELLA! CAN YOU HEAR ME!?
THE PERSON CAN HEAR YOU, BUT CAN'T RESPOND TO ANYTHING YOU ASK. IT'S LIKE GOING INTO A DREAM, BUT WITHOUT FALLING ASLEEP.
AND THEN, YOU'RE FINE!
DOCTORS AREN'T REALLY SURE WHAT CAUSES ABSENCE SEIZURES, BUT THEY KNOW THAT EXTRA ZAPPING ON BOTH SIDES OF THE BRAIN SEEMS TO BE A TRIGGER.

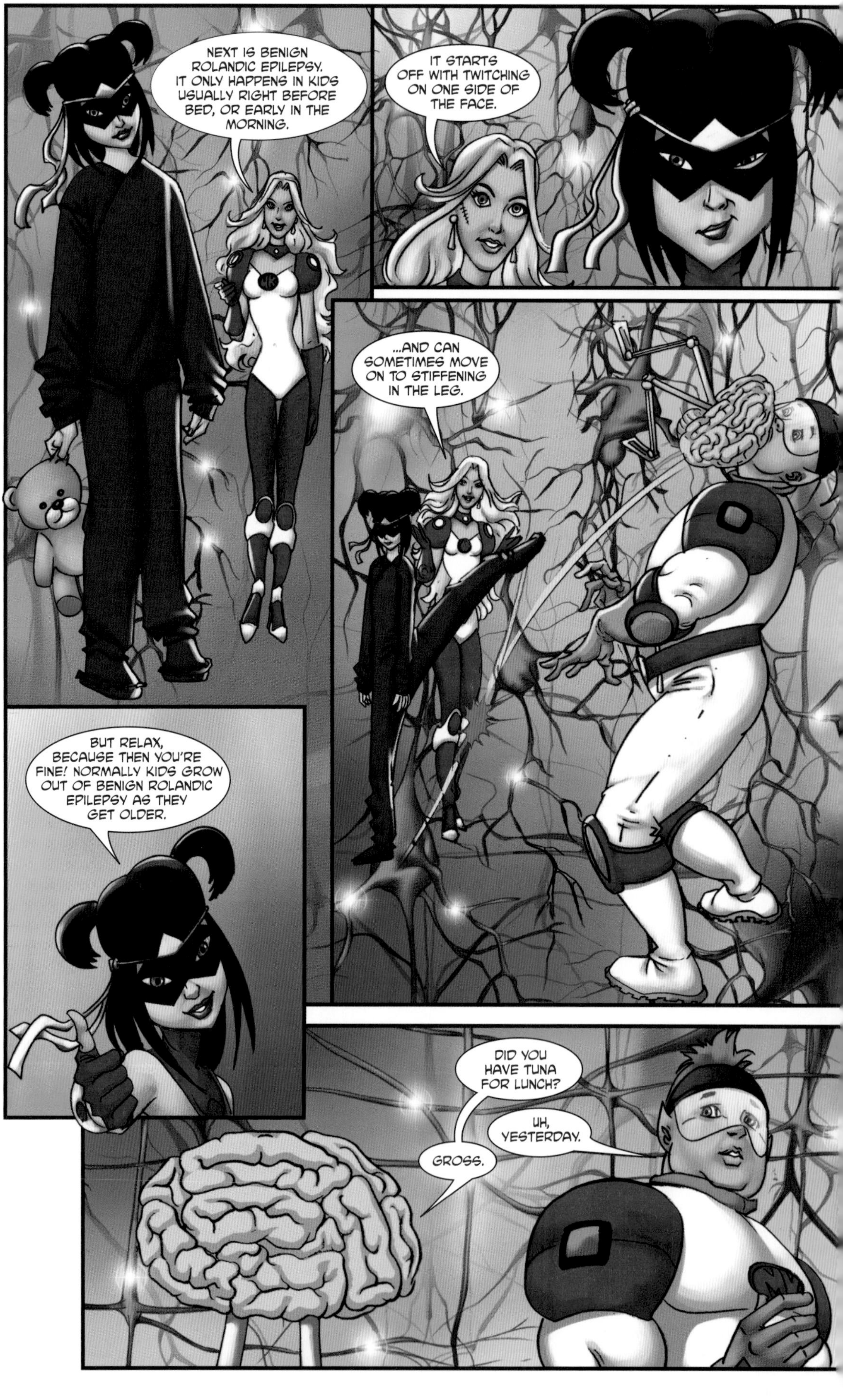
NEXT IS BENIGN ROLANDIC EPILEPSY. IT ONLY HAPPENS IN KIDS USUALLY RIGHT BEFORE BED, OR EARLY IN THE MORNING.
IT STARTS OFF WITH TWITCHING ON ONE SIDE OF THE FACE.
...AND CAN SOMETIMES MOVE ON TO STIFFENING IN THE LEG.
BUT RELAX, BECAUSE THEN YOU'RE FINE! NORMALLY KIDS GROW OUT OF BENIGN ROLANDIC EPILEPSY AS THEY GET OLDER.
DID YOU HAVE TUNA FOR LUNCH?
UH, YESTERDAY.
GROSS.

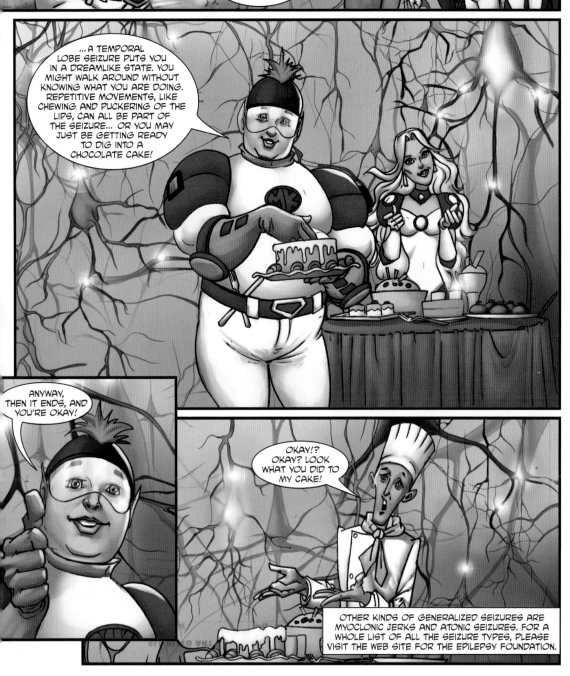

OK, MY TURN, MY TURN! ANOTHER COMMON SEIZURE IN KIDS IS THE TEMPORAL LOBE SEIZURE. REMEMBER THE NEURONS FROM THE TEMPORAL LOBE? WELL, ASIDE FROM HOUSING THE NEURONS THAT MAKE YOU SMELL..

AND PEOPLE SAY HE DOESN'T HAVE COMEDIC TIMING!

EXCUSE ME. EXTRA PEPPERONI GETS ME ALL THE TIME.

...A TEMPORAL LOBE SEIZURE PUTS YOU IN A DREAMLIKE STATE. YOU MIGHT WALK AROUND WITHOUT KNOWING WHAT YOU ARE DOING. REPETITIVE MOVEMENTS, LIKE CHEWING AND PUCKERING OF THE LIPS, CAN ALL BE PART OF THE SEIZURE... OR YOU MAY JUST BE GETTING READY TO DIG INTO A CHOCOLATE CAKE!

ANYWAY, THEN IT ENDS, AND YOU'RE OKAY!

OKAY!? OKAY? LOOK WHAT YOU DID TO MY CAKE!

OTHER KINDS OF GENERALIZED SEIZURES ARE MYOCLONIC JERKS AND ATONIC SEIZURES. FOR A WHOLE LIST OF ALL THE SEIZURE TYPES, PLEASE VISIT THE WEB SITE FOR THE EPILEPSY FOUNDATION.

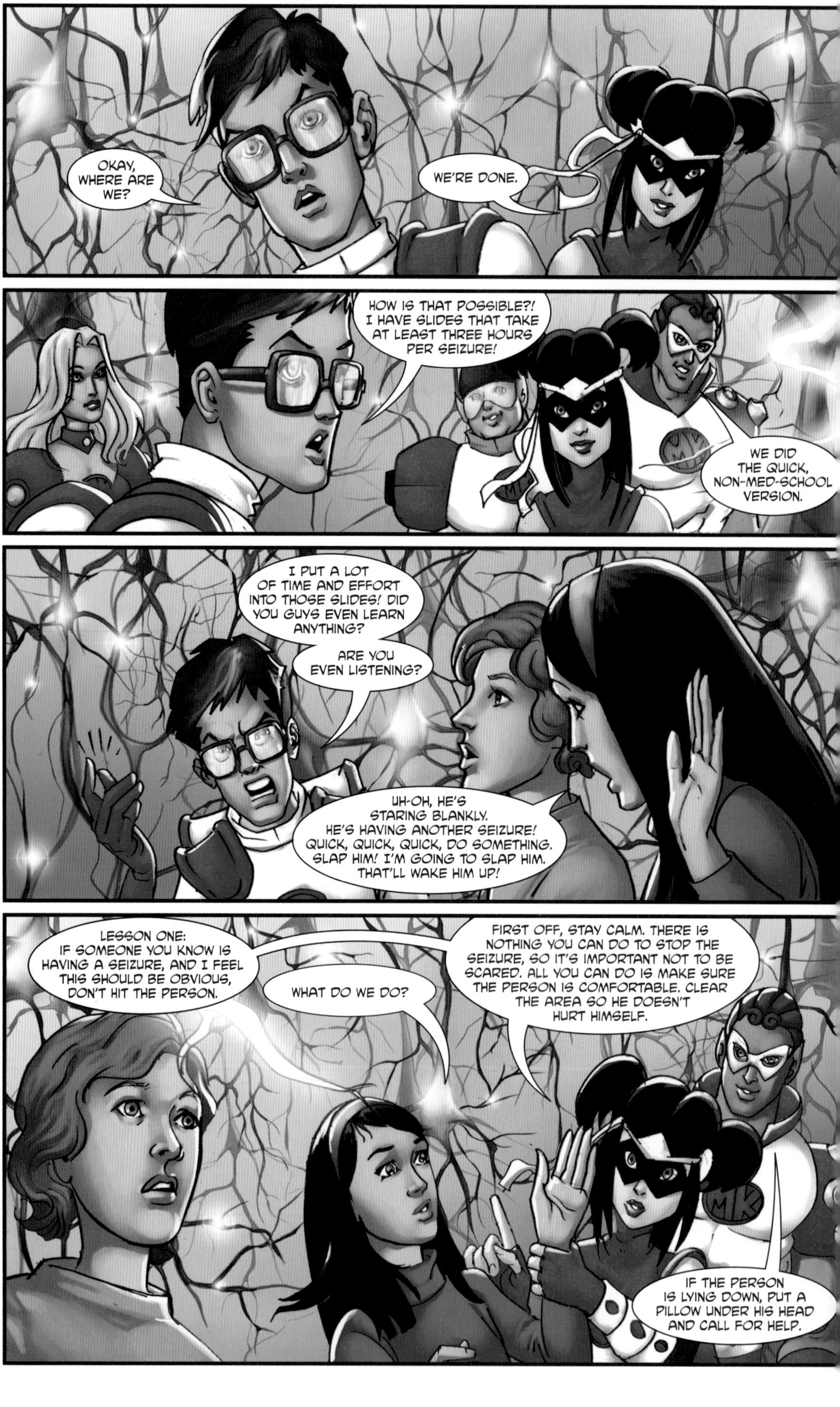
OKAY, WHERE ARE WE?
WE'RE DONE.
HOW IS THAT POSSIBLE?! I HAVE SLIDES THAT TAKE AT LEAST THREE HOURS PER SEIZURE!
WE DID THE QUICK, NON-MED-SCHOOL VERSION.
I PUT A LOT OF TIME AND EFFORT INTO THOSE SLIDES! DID YOU GUYS EVEN LEARN ANYTHING?
ARE YOU EVEN LISTENING?
UH-OH, HE'S STARING BLANKLY. HE'S HAVING ANOTHER SEIZURE! QUICK, QUICK, QUICK, DO SOMETHING. SLAP HIM! I'M GOING TO SLAP HIM. THAT'LL WAKE HIM UP!
LESSON ONE: IF SOMEONE YOU KNOW IS HAVING A SEIZURE, AND I FEEL THIS SHOULD BE OBVIOUS, DON'T HIT THE PERSON.
WHAT DO WE DO?
FIRST OFF, STAY CALM. THERE IS NOTHING YOU CAN DO TO STOP THE SEIZURE, SO IT'S IMPORTANT NOT TO BE SCARED. ALL YOU CAN DO IS MAKE SURE THE PERSON IS COMFORTABLE. CLEAR THE AREA SO HE DOESN'T HURT HIMSELF.
IF THE PERSON IS LYING DOWN, PUT A PILLOW UNDER HIS HEAD AND CALL FOR HELP.

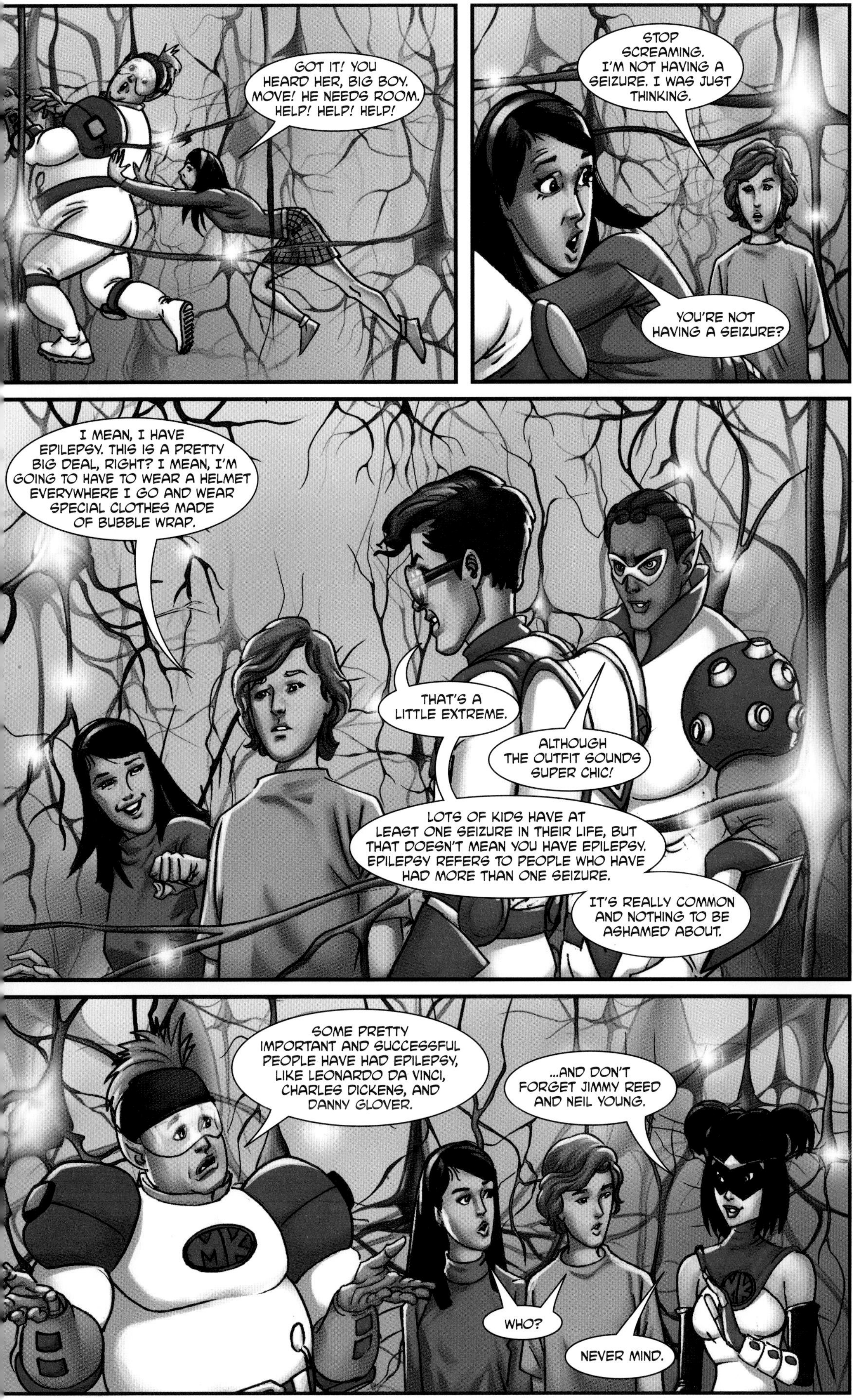
GOT IT! YOU HEARD HER, BIG BOY. MOVE! HE NEEDS ROOM. HELP! HELP! HELP!
STOP SCREAMING. I'M NOT HAVING A SEIZURE. I WAS JUST THINKING.
YOU'RE NOT HAVING A SEIZURE?
I MEAN, I HAVE EPILEPSY. THIS IS A PRETTY BIG DEAL, RIGHT? I MEAN, I'M GOING TO HAVE TO WEAR A HELMET EVERYWHERE I GO AND WEAR SPECIAL CLOTHES MADE OF BUBBLE WRAP.
THAT'S A LITTLE EXTREME.
ALTHOUGH THE OUTFIT SOUNDS SUPER CHIC!
LOTS OF KIDS HAVE AT LEAST ONE SEIZURE IN THEIR LIFE, BUT THAT DOESN'T MEAN YOU HAVE EPILEPSY. EPILEPSY REFERS TO PEOPLE WHO HAVE HAD MORE THAN ONE SEIZURE.
IT'S REALLY COMMON AND NOTHING TO BE ASHAMED ABOUT.
SOME PRETTY IMPORTANT AND SUCCESSFUL PEOPLE HAVE HAD EPILEPSY, LIKE LEONARDO DA VINCI, CHARLES DICKENS, AND DANNY GLOVER.
...AND DON'T FORGET JIMMY REED AND NEIL YOUNG.
WHO?
NEVER MIND.

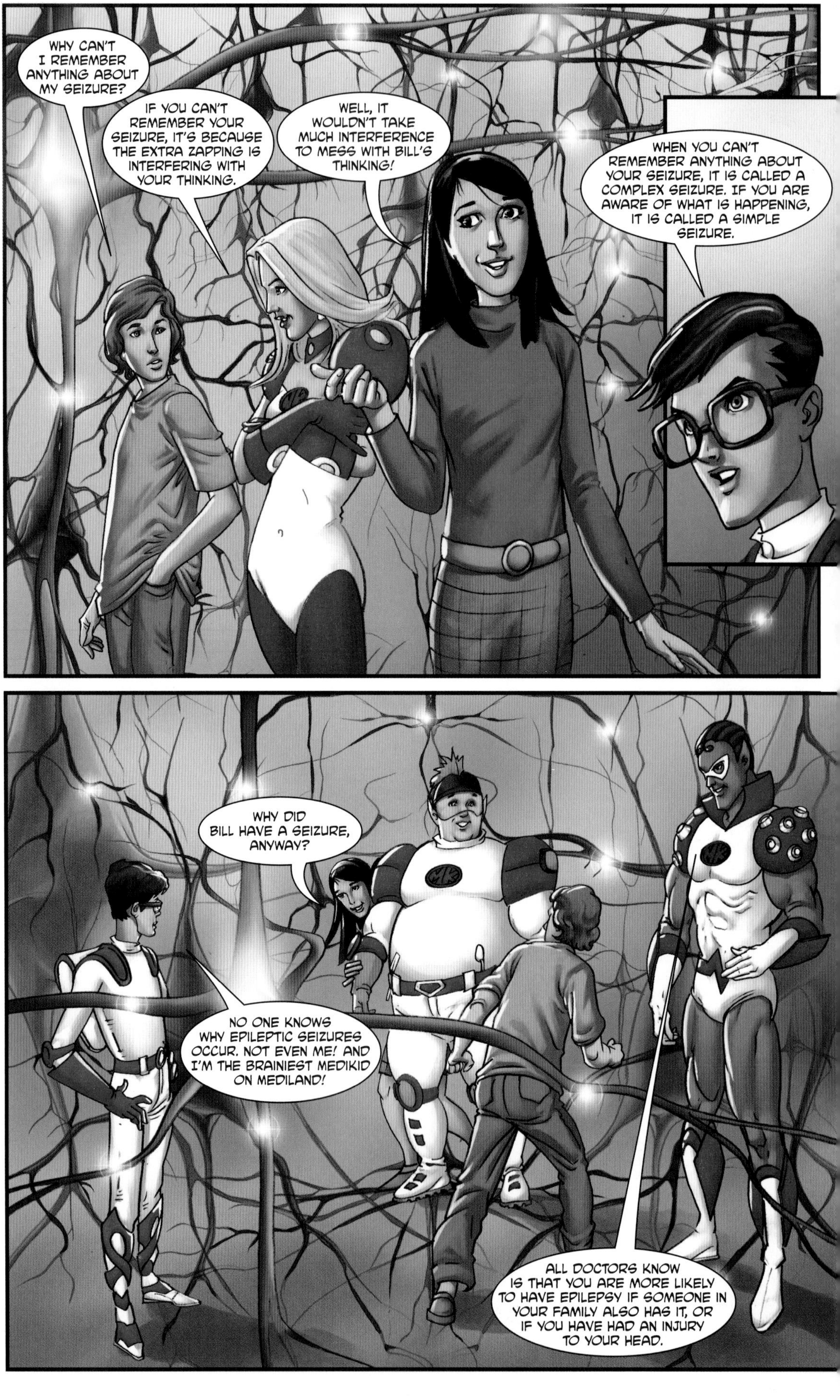

WHY CAN'T I REMEMBER ANYTHING ABOUT MY SEIZURE?
IF YOU CAN'T REMEMBER YOUR SEIZURE, IT'S BECAUSE THE EXTRA ZAPPING IS INTERFERING WITH YOUR THINKING.
WELL, IT WOULDN'T TAKE MUCH INTERFERENCE TO MESS WITH BILL'S THINKING!
WHEN YOU CAN'T REMEMBER ANYTHING ABOUT YOUR SEIZURE, IT IS CALLED A COMPLEX SEIZURE. IF YOU ARE AWARE OF WHAT IS HAPPENING, IT IS CALLED A SIMPLE SEIZURE.
WHY DID BILL HAVE A SEIZURE, ANYWAY?
NO ONE KNOWS WHY EPILEPTIC SEIZURES OCCUR. NOT EVEN ME! AND I'M THE BRAINIEST MEDIKID ON MEDILAND!
ALL DOCTORS KNOW IS THAT YOU ARE MORE LIKELY TO HAVE EPILEPSY IF SOMEONE IN YOUR FAMILY ALSO HAS IT, OR IF YOU HAVE HAD AN INJURY TO YOUR HEAD.

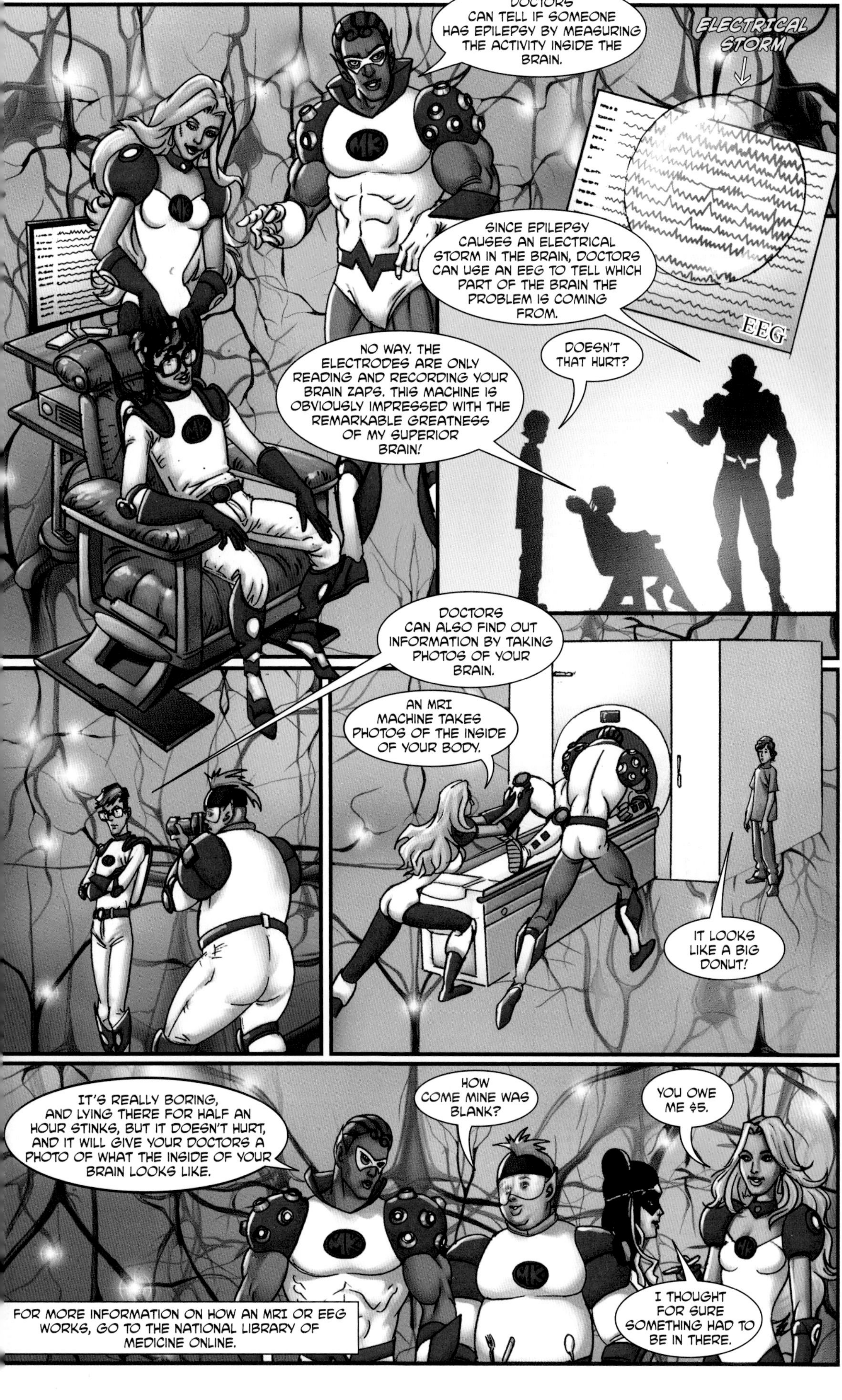
DOCTORS CAN TELL IF SOMEONE HAS EPILEPSY BY MEASURING THE ACTIVITY INSIDE THE BRAIN.
ELECTRICAL STORM
EEG
SINCE EPILEPSY CAUSES AN ELECTRICAL STORM IN THE BRAIN, DOCTORS CAN USE AN EEG TO TELL WHICH PART OF THE BRAIN THE PROBLEM IS COMING FROM.
DOESN'T THAT HURT?
NO WAY. THE ELECTRODES ARE ONLY READING AND RECORDING YOUR BRAIN ZAPS. THIS MACHINE IS OBVIOUSLY IMPRESSED WITH THE REMARKABLE GREATNESS OF MY SUPERIOR BRAIN!
DOCTORS CAN ALSO FIND OUT INFORMATION BY TAKING PHOTOS OF YOUR BRAIN.
AN MRI MACHINE TAKES PHOTOS OF THE INSIDE OF YOUR BODY.
IT LOOKS LIKE A BIG DONUT!
IT'S REALLY BORING, AND LYING THERE FOR HALF AN HOUR STINKS, BUT IT DOESN'T HURT, AND IT WILL GIVE YOUR DOCTORS A PHOTO OF WHAT THE INSIDE OF YOUR BRAIN LOOKS LIKE.
HOW COME MINE WAS BLANK?
YOU OWE ME $5.
I THOUGHT FOR SURE SOMETHING HAD TO BE IN THERE.
FOR MORE INFORMATION ON HOW AN MRI OR EEG WORKS, GO TO THE NATIONAL LIBRARY OF MEDICINE ONLINE.

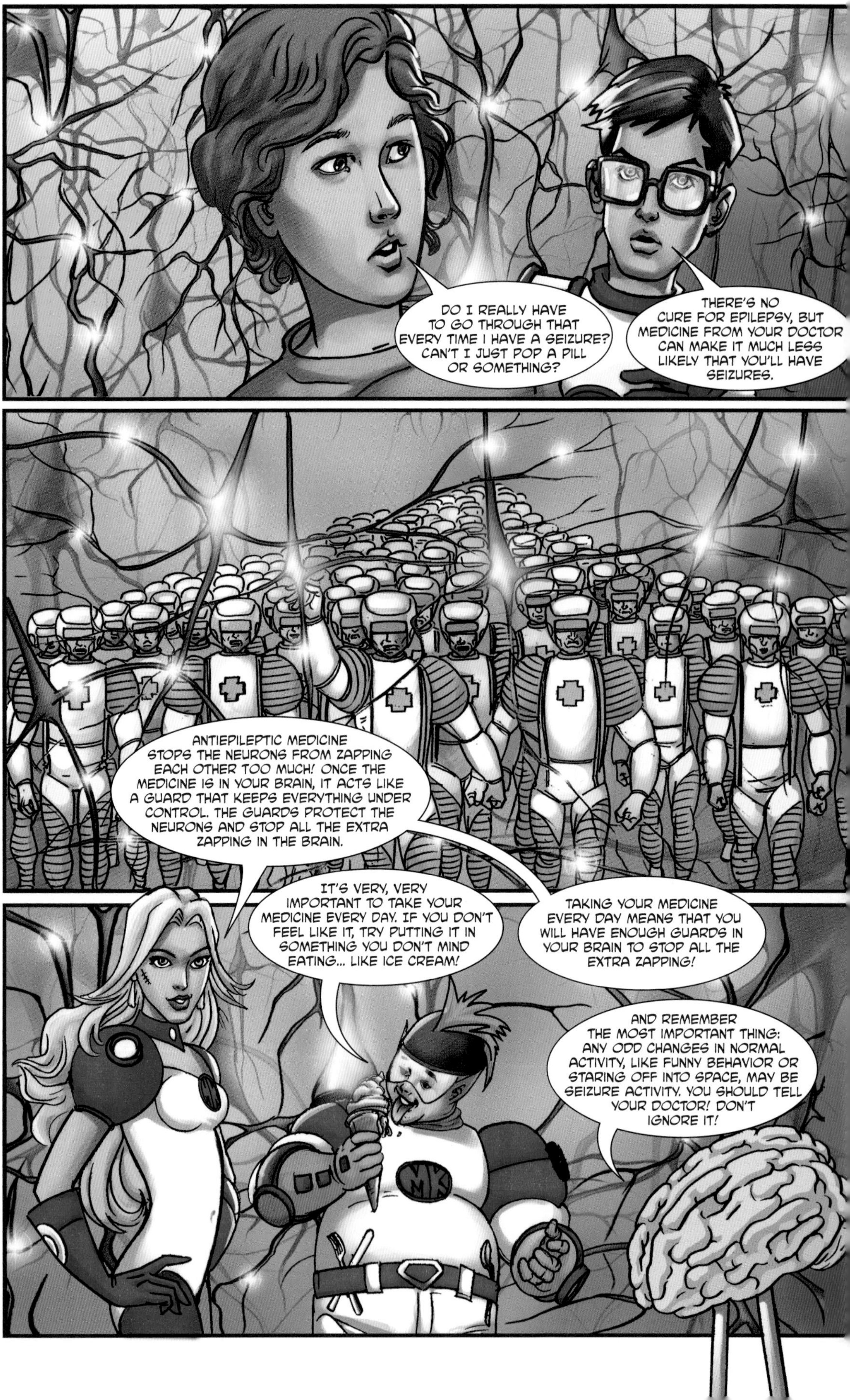
DO I REALLY HAVE TO GO THROUGH THAT EVERY TIME I HAVE A SEIZURE? CAN'T I JUST POP A PILL OR SOMETHING?
THERE'S NO CURE FOR EPILEPSY, BUT MEDICINE FROM YOUR DOCTOR CAN MAKE IT MUCH LESS LIKELY THAT YOU'LL HAVE SEIZURES.
ANTIEPILEPTIC MEDICINE STOPS THE NEURONS FROM ZAPPING EACH OTHER TOO MUCH! ONCE THE MEDICINE IS IN YOUR BRAIN, IT ACTS LIKE A GUARD THAT KEEPS EVERYTHING UNDER CONTROL. THE GUARDS PROTECT THE NEURONS AND STOP ALL THE EXTRA ZAPPING IN THE BRAIN.
IT'S VERY, VERY IMPORTANT TO TAKE YOUR MEDICINE EVERY DAY. IF YOU DON'T FEEL LIKE IT, TRY PUTTING IT IN SOMETHING YOU DON'T MIND EATING... LIKE ICE CREAM!
TAKING YOUR MEDICINE EVERY DAY MEANS THAT YOU WILL HAVE ENOUGH GUARDS IN YOUR BRAIN TO STOP ALL THE EXTRA ZAPPING!
AND REMEMBER THE MOST IMPORTANT THING: ANY ODD CHANGES IN NORMAL ACTIVITY, LIKE FUNNY BEHAVIOR OR STARING OFF INTO SPACE, MAY BE SEIZURE ACTIVITY. YOU SHOULD TELL YOUR DOCTOR! DON'T IGNORE IT!

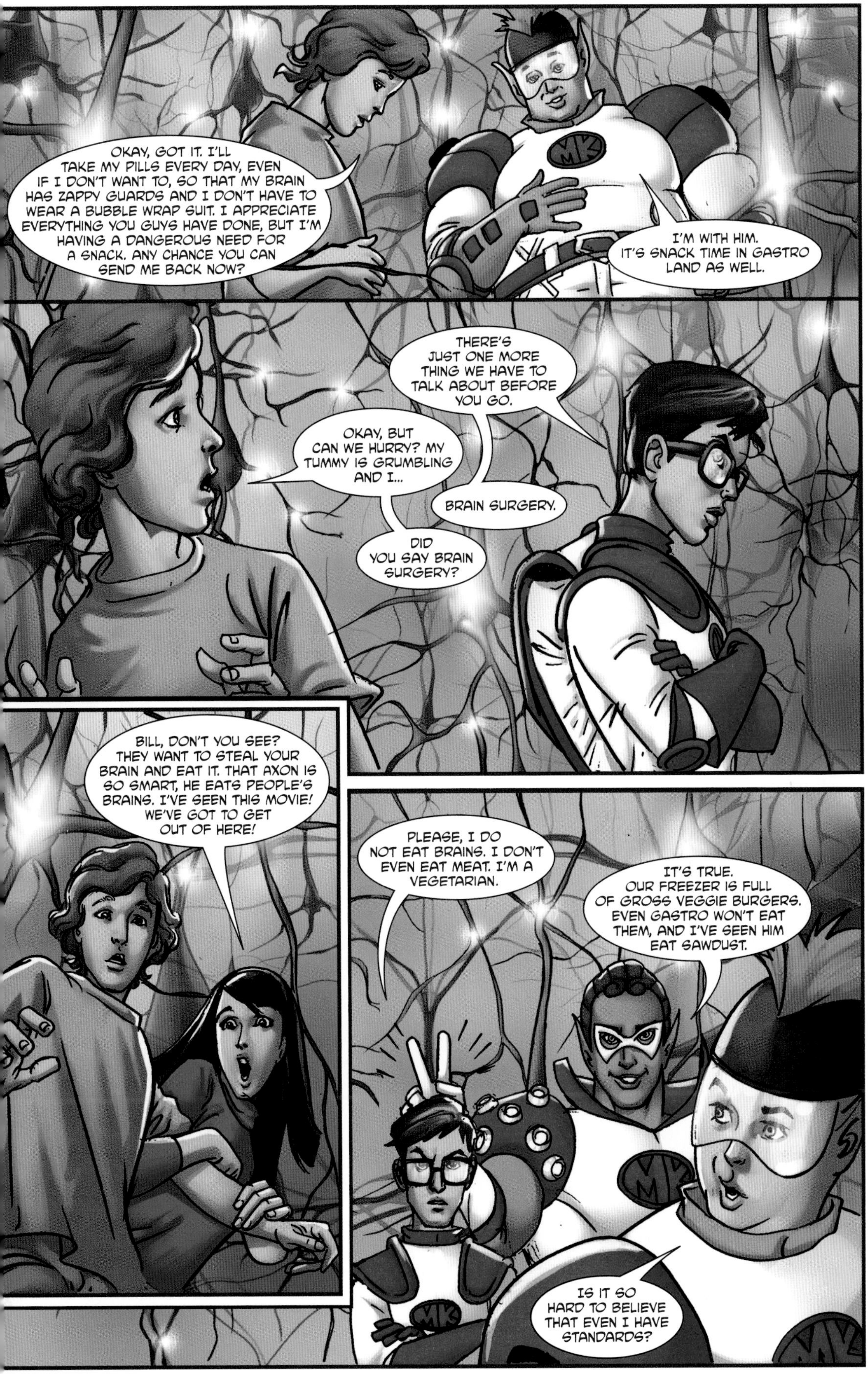
OKAY, GOT IT. I'LL TAKE MY PILLS EVERY DAY, EVEN IF I DON'T WANT TO, SO THAT MY BRAIN HAS ZAPPY GUARDS AND I DON'T HAVE TO WEAR A BUBBLE WRAP SUIT. I APPRECIATE EVERYTHING YOU GUYS HAVE DONE, BUT I'M HAVING A DANGEROUS NEED FOR A SNACK. ANY CHANCE YOU CAN SEND ME BACK NOW?
I'M WITH HIM. IT'S SNACK TIME IN GASTRO LAND AS WELL.
THERE'S JUST ONE MORE THING WE HAVE TO TALK ABOUT BEFORE YOU GO.
OKAY, BUT CAN WE HURRY? MY TUMMY IS GRUMBLING AND I...
BRAIN SURGERY.
DID YOU SAY BRAIN SURGERY?
BILL, DON'T YOU SEE? THEY WANT TO STEAL YOUR BRAIN AND EAT IT. THAT AXON IS SO SMART, HE EATS PEOPLE'S BRAINS. I'VE SEEN THIS MOVIE! WE'VE GOT TO GET OUT OF HERE!
PLEASE, I DO NOT EAT BRAINS. I DON'T EVEN EAT MEAT. I'M A VEGETARIAN.
IT'S TRUE. OUR FREEZER IS FULL OF GROSS VEGGIE BURGERS. EVEN GASTRO WON'T EAT THEM, AND I'VE SEEN HIM EAT SAWDUST.
IS IT SO HARD TO BELIEVE THAT EVEN I HAVE STANDARDS?

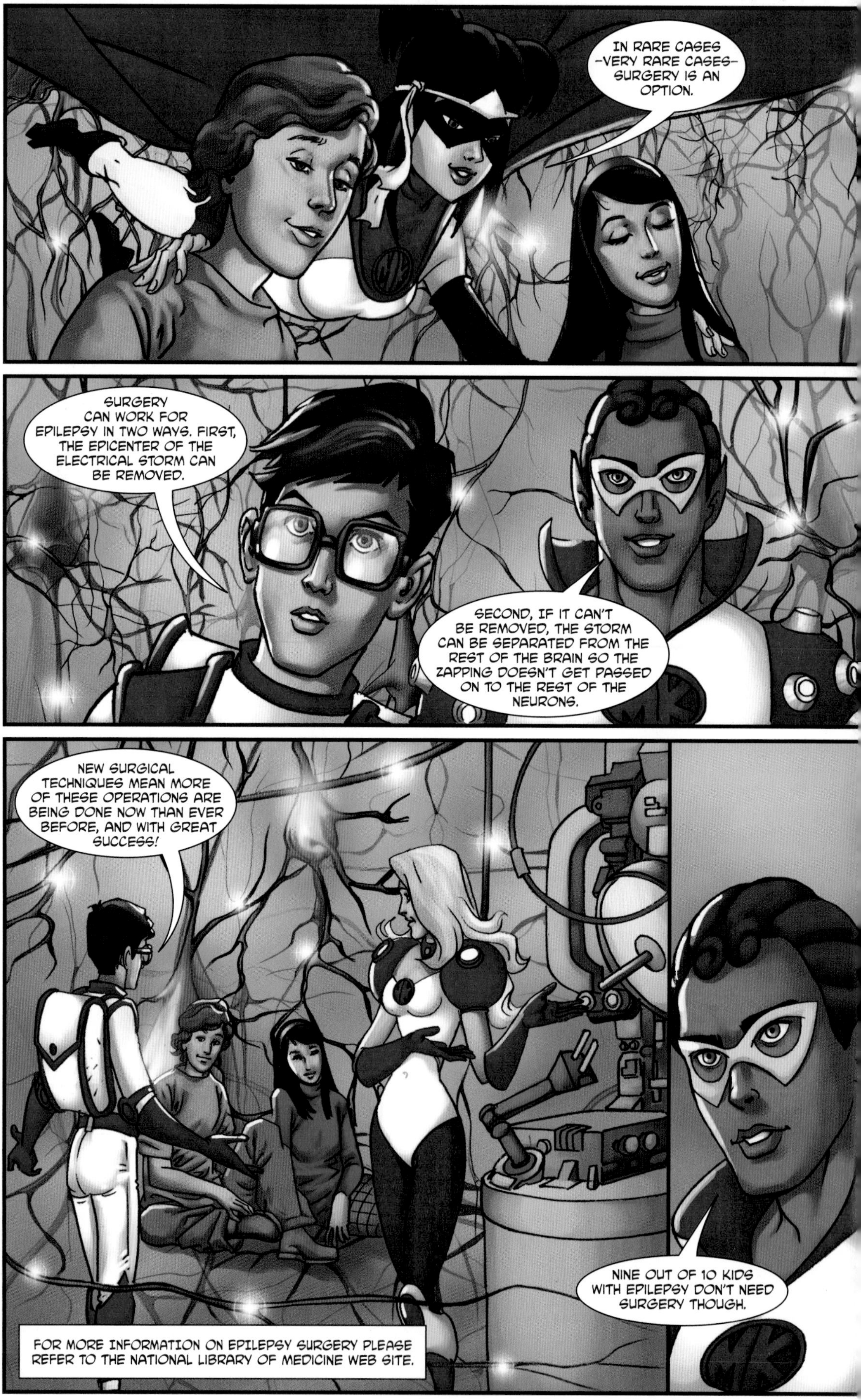

IN RARE CASES —VERY RARE CASES— SURGERY IS AN OPTION.
SURGERY CAN WORK FOR EPILEPSY IN TWO WAYS. FIRST, THE EPICENTER OF THE ELECTRICAL STORM CAN BE REMOVED.
SECOND, IF IT CAN'T BE REMOVED, THE STORM CAN BE SEPARATED FROM THE REST OF THE BRAIN SO THE ZAPPING DOESN'T GET PASSED ON TO THE REST OF THE NEURONS.
NEW SURGICAL TECHNIQUES MEAN MORE OF THESE OPERATIONS ARE BEING DONE NOW THAN EVER BEFORE, AND WITH GREAT SUCCESS!
NINE OUT OF 10 KIDS WITH EPILEPSY DON'T NEED SURGERY THOUGH.
FOR MORE INFORMATION ON EPILEPSY SURGERY PLEASE REFER TO THE NATIONAL LIBRARY OF MEDICINE WEB SITE.

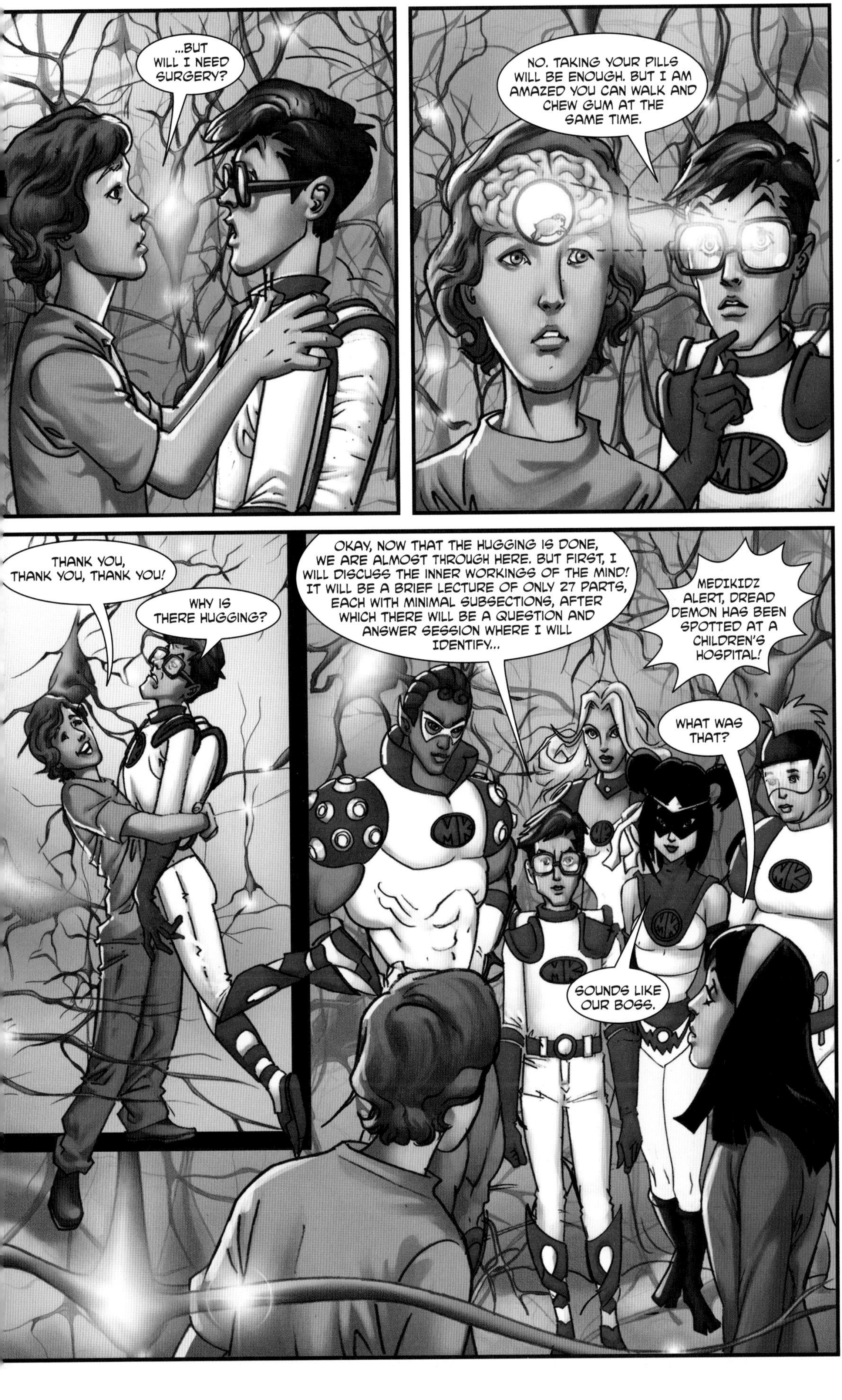
...BUT WILL I NEED SURGERY?
NO. TAKING YOUR PILLS WILL BE ENOUGH. BUT I AM AMAZED YOU CAN WALK AND CHEW GUM AT THE SAME TIME.
THANK YOU, THANK YOU, THANK YOU!
WHY IS THERE HUGGING?
OKAY, NOW THAT THE HUGGING IS DONE, WE ARE ALMOST THROUGH HERE. BUT FIRST, I WILL DISCUSS THE INNER WORKINGS OF THE MIND! IT WILL BE A BRIEF LECTURE OF ONLY 27 PARTS, EACH WITH MINIMAL SUBSECTIONS, AFTER WHICH THERE WILL BE A QUESTION AND ANSWER SESSION WHERE I WILL IDENTIFY...
MEDIKIDZ ALERT, DREAD DEMON HAS BEEN SPOTTED AT A CHILDREN'S HOSPITAL!
WHAT WAS THAT?
SOUNDS LIKE OUR BOSS.

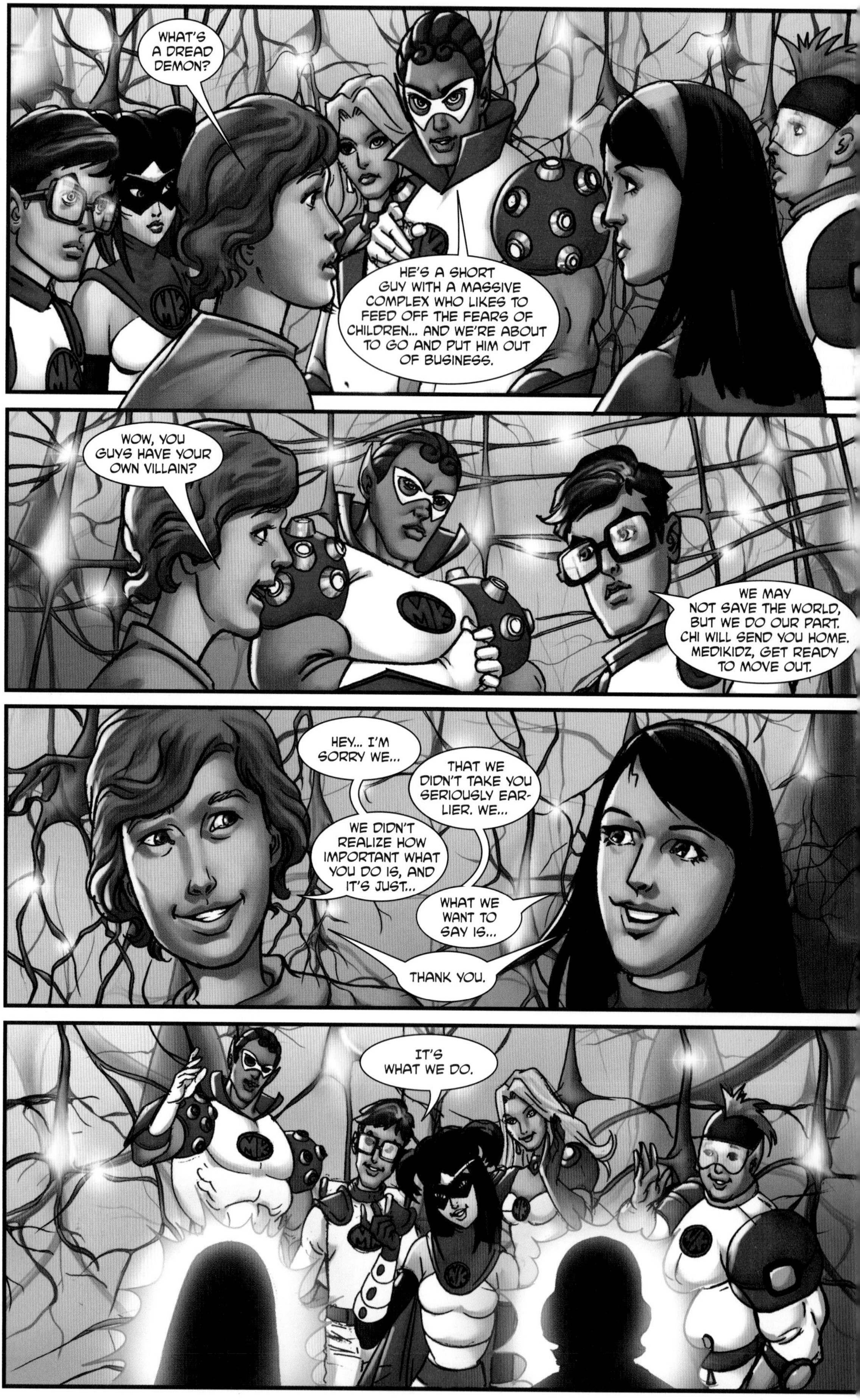
WHAT'S A DREAD DEMON?
HE'S A SHORT GUY WITH A MASSIVE COMPLEX WHO LIKES TO FEED OFF THE FEARS OF CHILDREN... AND WE'RE ABOUT TO GO AND PUT HIM OUT OF BUSINESS.
WOW, YOU GUYS HAVE YOUR OWN VILLAIN?
WE MAY NOT SAVE THE WORLD, BUT WE DO OUR PART. CHI WILL SEND YOU HOME. MEDIKIDZ, GET READY TO MOVE OUT.
HEY... I'M SORRY WE...
THAT WE DIDN'T TAKE YOU SERIOUSLY EAR-LIER. WE...
WE DIDN'T REALIZE HOW IMPORTANT WHAT YOU DO IS, AND IT'S JUST...
WHAT WE WANT TO SAY IS...
THANK YOU.
IT'S WHAT WE DO.

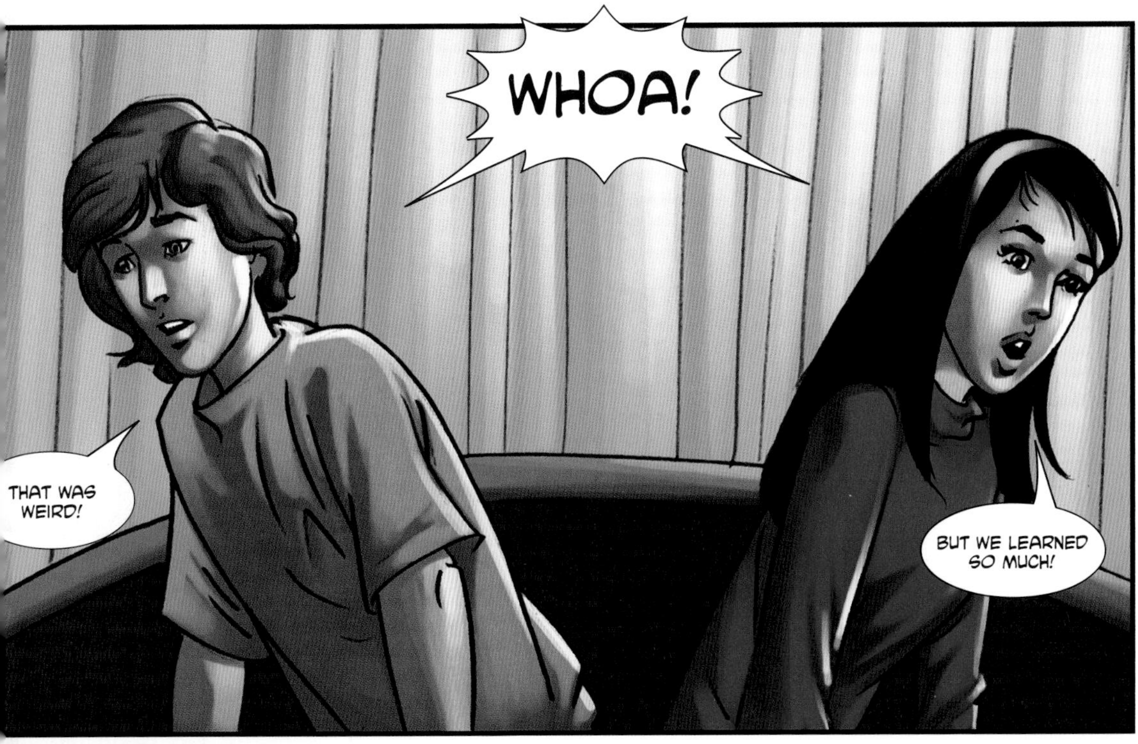
WHOA!
THAT WAS WEIRD!
BUT WE LEARNED SO MUCH!

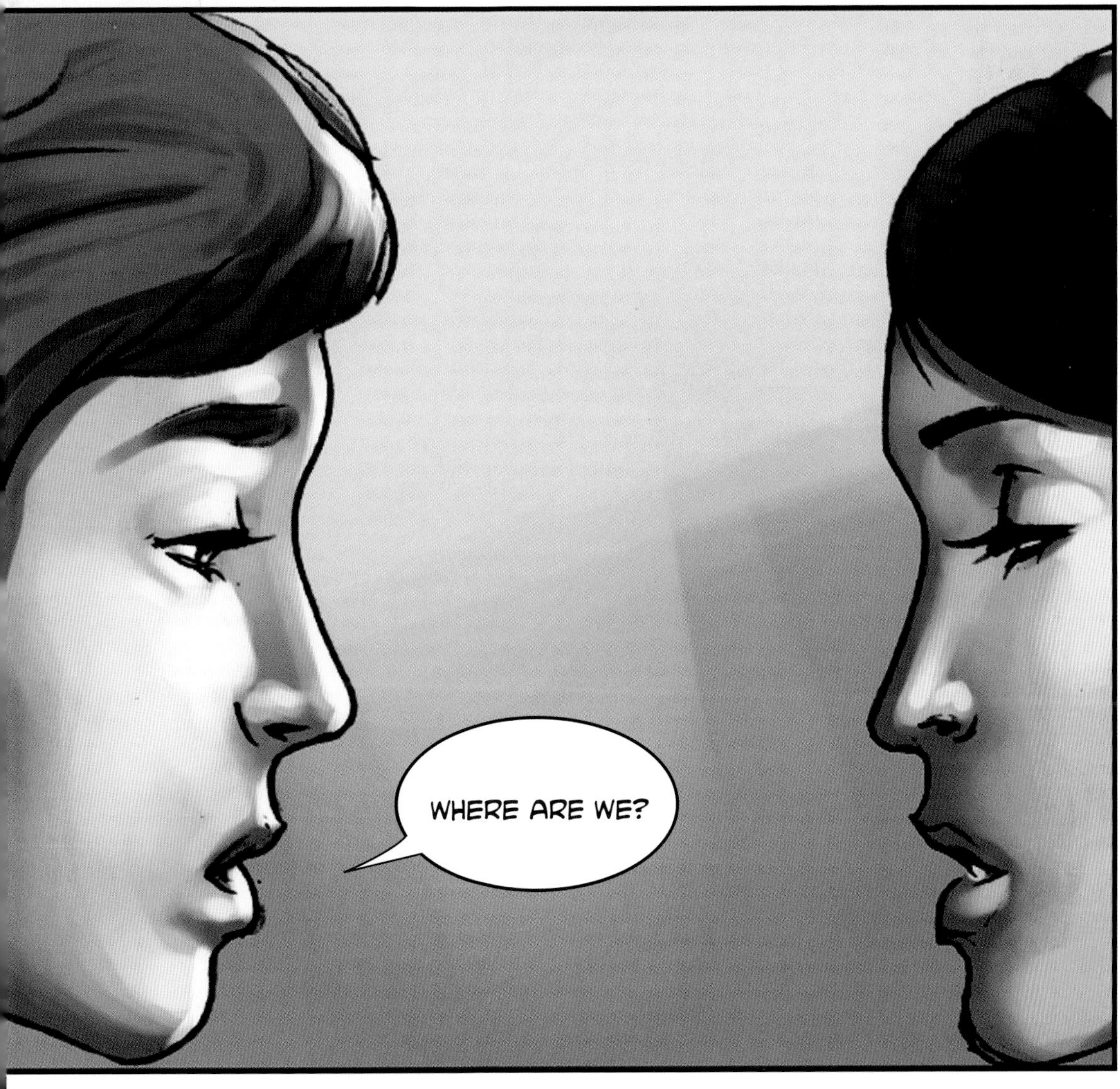
WHERE ARE WE?

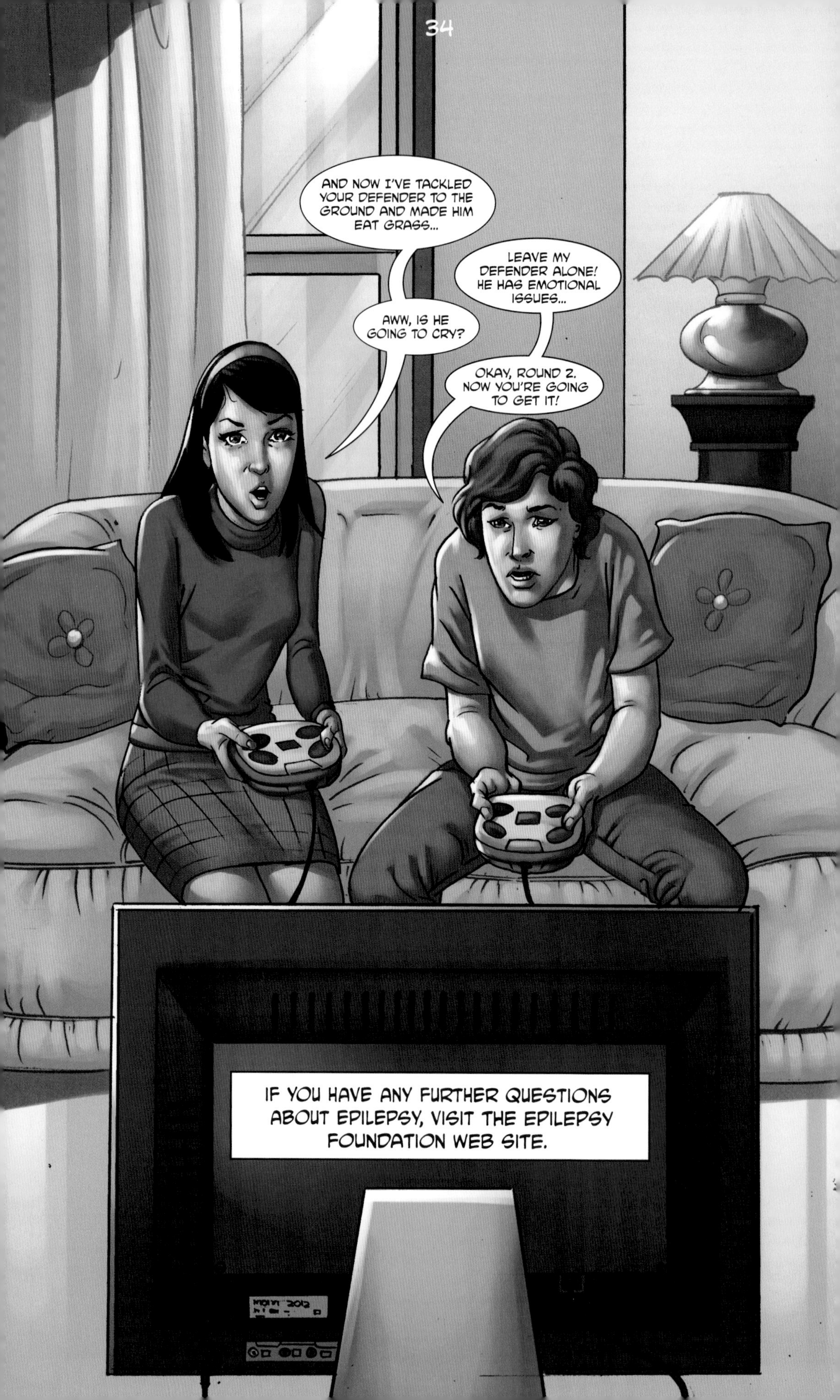
AND NOW I'VE TACKLED YOUR DEFENDER TO THE GROUND AND MADE HIM EAT GRASS...
LEAVE MY DEFENDER ALONE! HE HAS EMOTIONAL ISSUES...
AWW, IS HE GOING TO CRY?
OKAY, ROUND 2. NOW YOU'RE GOING TO GET IT!
IF YOU HAVE ANY FURTHER QUESTIONS ABOUT EPILEPSY, VISIT THE EPILEPSY FOUNDATION WEB SITE.

GLOSSARY

ABSENCE SEIZURE A TYPE OF GENERALIZED SEIZURE WHERE
    THERE IS A BRIEF, SUDDEN LAPSE OF CONSCIOUS ACTIVITY.
    THE PERSON MAY APPEAR TO BE STARING INTO SPACE.

ATONIC SEIZURE A TYPE OF GENERALIZED SEIZURE THAT CON-
    SISTS OF A BRIEF LAPSE IN MUSCLE TENSION, USUALLY
    CAUSING THE PERSON TO FALL TO THE GROUND.

AURA A DISTINCT FEELING OR WARNING SIGN THAT A SEIZURE IS
    COMING. THIS CAN INCLUDE A CHANGE TO BODILY SENSATIONS,
    LIKE STRANGE SMELLS OR LIGHTS.

BENIGN ROLANDIC EPILEPSY THE MOST COMMON TYPE OF EPI-
    LEPSY SYNDROME IN CHILDHOOD, ALTHOUGH MOST CHILDREN
    OUTGROW IT. SEIZURES ARE EITHER SIMPLE PARTIAL OR
    GENERALIZED TONIC-CLONIC.

BRAIN THE CENTER OF THE HUMAN NERVOUS SYSTEM, CON-
    TROLLING THOUGHT, INVOLUNTARY MOVEMENT IN THE BODY,
    BALANCE, GROWTH, AND TEMPERATURE CONTROL.

COMPLEX SEIZURE A SEIZURE THAT IS LIMITED TO ONE CERE-
    BRAL HEMISPHERE AND CAUSES IMPAIRMENT OF AWARENESS
    OR RESPONSIVENESS.

ELECTROENCEPHALOGRAPHY (EEG) A TEST TO DETECT PROB-
    LEMS IN THE ELECTRICAL ACTIVITY OF THE BRAIN. ELECTRODES
    ARE ATTACHED TO THE SCALP TO MEASURE FAINT ELECTRICAL
    ACTIVITY AND A RECORDING MACHINE CONVERTS THE ELECTRI-
    CAL IMPULSES INTO PATTERNS THAT CAN BE SEEN ON A
    COMPUTER SCREEN.

EPILEPSY A BRAIN DISORDER INVOLVING REPEATED, SPONTANE-
    OUS SEIZURES CAUSED BY ABNORMALLY EXCITED ELECTRICAL
    SIGNALS IN THE BRAIN.

FOCAL (PARTIAL) SEIZURE A TYPE OF SEIZURE WHERE THE
    ELECTRICAL ACTIVITY REMAINS IN A LIMITED AREA OF
    THE BRAIN.

FRONTAL LOBE THE PART OF THE BRAIN LOCATED AT THE FRONT
    OF EACH CEREBRAL HEMISPHERE. IT IS ASSOCIATED WITH
    REASONING, PLANNING, PARTS OF SPEECH AND MOVEMENT,
    EMOTIONS, AND PROBLEM-SOLVING.

GENERALIZED SEIZURE SEIZURES THAT AFFECT BOTH CEREBRAL
    HEMISPHERES AND CAN CAUSE LOSS OF CONSCIOUSNESS.

MAGNETIC RESONANCE IMAGING (MRI) A SCANNING TECHNIQUE
    WHERE A POWERFUL MAGNETIC FIELD AND RADIO FREQUENCY
    PULSES ARE USED TO CREATE DETAILED IMAGES OF THE
    INSIDE OF THE BODY.

MYOCLONIC SEIZURE A TYPE OF GENERALIZED SEIZURE
    CHARACTERIZED BY RAPID, BRIEF CONTRACTIONS OF BODILY

MUSCLES, WHICH USUALLY OCCUR ON BOTH SIDES OF THE BODY AT THE SAME TIME, BUT CAN OCCASIONALLY JUST INCLUDE ONE FOOT OR ARM.

NEURONS CELLS OF THE NERVOUS SYSTEM, SPECIALIZED TO CARRY "MESSAGES" TO AND FROM THE BRAIN TO OTHER PARTS OF THE BODY.

OCCIPITAL LOBE THE PART OF THE BRAIN LOCATED IN THE REARMOST PORTION OF THE SKULL. IT ACTS AS THE VISUAL PROCESSING CENTER OF THE BRAIN.

PARIETAL LOBE THE PART OF THE BRAIN LOCATED ABOVE THE OCCIPITAL LOBE AND BEHIND THE FRONTAL LOBE. IT IS CONCERNED WITH STIMULI RELATED TO TOUCH, PRESSURE, TEMPERATURE, AND PAIN.

SEIZURE A LOSS OF AWARENESS OR CONSCIOUSNESS CAUSED BY ABNORMAL ELECTRICAL DISCHARGES IN THE BRAIN.

TEMPORAL LOBE THE PART OF THE BRAIN LOCATED ON BOTH THE RIGHT AND LEFT SIDES. IT IS CONCERNED WITH HEARING AND MEMORY.

TONIC-CLONIC SEIZURE THE MOST COMMON AND BEST KNOWN TYPE OF GENERALIZED SEIZURE. IT IS CHARACTERIZED BY A STIFFENING OF THE LIMBS, FOLLOWED BY JERKING OF THE FACE AND LIMBS.

FOR MORE INFORMATION

CHARLIE FOUNDATION TO HELP CURE PEDIATRIC EPILEPSY
1223 WILSHIRE BOULEVARD, SUITE 815
SANTA MONICA, CA 90403
(310) 393-2347
WEB SITE: HTTP://WWW.CHARLIEFOUNDATION.ORG
A FOUNDATION DEDICATED TO FINDING A CURE FOR EPILEPSY.

CITIZENS UNITED FOR RESEARCH IN EPILEPSY
730 NORTH FRANKLIN STREET, SUITE 404
CHICAGO, IL 60654
(312) 255-1801
WEB SITE: HTTP://WWW.CUREEPILEPSY.ORG
A NONPROFIT ORGANIZATION DEDICATED TO FINDING A CURE
    FOR EPILEPSY BY RAISING FUNDS FOR RESEARCH AND BY
    INCREASING AWARENESS OF THIS DISEASE.

EPILEPSY FOUNDATION OF AMERICA
8301 PROFESSIONAL PLACE
LANDOVER, MD 20785
(800) 332-1000
WEB SITE: HTTP://WWW.EPILEPSYFOUNDATION.ORG
A NATIONAL AGENCY DEDICATED TO THE WELFARE OF THE MORE
    THAN THREE MILLION PEOPLE WITH EPILEPSY IN THE UNITED
    STATES AND THEIR FAMILIES. THE FOUNDATION WORKS
    TOWARD IMPROVING LIVES AND WORKING TOWARD A CURE.

EPILEPSY THERAPY PROJECT
P.O. BOX 742
MIDDLEBURG, VA 20118
(540) 687-8077
WEB SITE: HTTP://WWW.EPILEPSY.COM
A NONPROFIT CORPORATION DEDICATED TO OVERCOMING THE
    FUNDING GAPS AND ROADBLOCKS THAT SLOW THE PROG-
    RESS OF NEW THERAPIES FROM THE LAB TO THE PATIENT.

NATIONAL ORGANIZATION FOR RARE DISORDERS
P.O. BOX 1968
DANBURY, CT 06813
(203) 744-0100
WEB SITE: HTTP://WWW.RAREDISEASES.ORG
AN ORGANIZATION DEDICATED TO HELPING PEOPLE WITH RARE
    DISEASES AND ASSISTING THE ORGANIZATIONS THAT
    SERVE THEM.

PEOPLE AGAINST CHILDHOOD EPILEPSY
7 EAST 85TH STREET, SUITE A3
NEW YORK, NY 10028
(212) 665-7223
WEB SITE: HTTP://WWW.PACEUSA.ORG
AN ORGANIZATION PROMOTING AWARENESS OF CHILDHOOD
    EPILEPSY AND OFFERING SUPPORT TO CHILDREN SUFFERING
    FROM IT.

WEB SITES

DUE TO THE CHANGING NATURE OF INTERNET LINKS, ROSEN
PUBLISHING HAS DEVELOPED AN ONLINE LIST OF WEB SITES
RELATED TO THE SUBJECT OF THIS BOOK. THIS SITE IS UPDATED
REGULARLY. PLEASE USE THIS LINK TO ACCESS THE LIST:

HTTP://WWW.ROSENLINKS.COM/MED/EPIL

ALARCON, GONZALO, LINA NASHEF, HELEN CROSS, JENNIFER NIGHTINGALE, AND STUART RICHARDSON. *EPILEPSY*. NEW YORK, NY: OXFORD, 2009.

BAZIL, CARL W. *LIVING WELL WITH EPILEPSY AND OTHER SEIZURE DISORDERS: AN EXPERT EXPLAINS WHAT YOU REALLY NEED TO KNOW*. NEW YORK, NY: HARPER PAPERBACKS, 2004.

BLACKBURN, LYNN BENNETT. *GROWING UP WITH EPILEPSY: A PRACTICAL GUIDE FOR PARENTS*. NEW YORK, NY: DEMOS MEDICAL PUBLISHING, 2003.

BROWNE, THOMAS R., AND GREGORY L. HOLMES. *HANDBOOK OF EPILEPSY*. PHILADELPHIA, PA: LIPPINCOTT WILLIAMS & WILKINS, 2008.

DEVINSKY, ORRIN. *EPILEPSY: PATIENT AND FAMILY GUIDE*. 3RD ED. NEW YORK, NY: DEMOS MEDICAL PUBLISHING, 2007.

FLETCHER, SALLY. *THE CHALLENGE OF EPILEPSY*. PHILADELPHIA, PA: AURA PUBLISHING, 2004.

FREEMAN, JOHN M., ERIC H. KOSSOFF, JENNIFER B. FREEMAN, AND MILLICENT T. KELLY. *THE KETOGENIC DIET: A TREATMENT FOR CHILDREN AND OTHERS WITH EPILEPSY*. NEW YORK, NY: DEMOS MEDICAL PUBLISHING, 2006.

GAY, KATHLYN. *EPILEPSY: THE ULTIMATE TEEN GUIDE*. LANHAM, MD: SCARECROW PRESS, 2007.

KRISHNAMURTHY, KAARKUZHALI BABU. *EPILEPSY IN OUR LIVES: WOMEN LIVING WITH EPILEPSY*. NEW YORK, NY: OXFORD, 2007.

LEPPIK, ILO E. *EPILEPSY: A GUIDE TO BALANCING YOUR LIFE*. NEW YORK, NY: DEMOS MEDICAL PUBLISHING, 2006.

PANAYIOTOPOULOS, C.P. *THE EPILEPSIES: SEIZURES, SYNDROMES AND MANAGEMENT*. OXFORDSHIRE, ENGLAND: BLADON MEDICAL PUBLISHING, 2004.

REUBER, MARKUS, M.D., CHRISTIAN E. ELGER, M.D., AND STEVEN C. SCHACHTER, M.D. *EPILEPSY EXPLAINED: A BOOK FOR PEOPLE WHO WANT TO KNOW MORE*. NEW YORK, NY: OXFORD, 2009.

SCHACHTER, STEVEN C. *EPILEPSY IN OUR WORDS: PERSONAL ACCOUNTS OF LIVING WITH SEIZURES*. NEW YORK, NY: OXFORD, 2007.

SHORVON, SIMON D. *HANDBOOK OF EPILEPSY TREATMENT*. HOBOKEN, NJ: WILEY, 2005.

SINGH, ANURADHA. *100 QUESTIONS & ANSWERS*. SUDBURY, MA: JONES AND BARTLETT, 2006.

WILNER, ANDREW N. *EPILEPSY: 100 ANSWERS: A DOCTOR RESPONDS TO HIS PATIENTS' QUESTIONS*. NEW YORK, NY: DEMOS MEDICAL PUBLISHING, 2007.

WYLLIE, ELAINE. *EPILEPSY: A CLEVELAND CLINIC GUIDE*. CLEVELAND, OH: CLEVELAND CLINIC PRESS, 2007.

INDEX

ABOUT THE AUTHORS

DR. KIM CHILMAN-BLAIR IS A MEDICAL DOCTOR WITH TEN YEARS' EXPERIENCE OF MEDICAL WRITING, AND A PASSION FOR PROVIDING MEDICAL INFORMATION THAT MAKES CHILDREN WANT TO LEARN.

JOHN TADDEO, FORMALLY OF MARVEL ENTERTAINMENT, IS A CELEBRATED COMIC BOOK WRITER AND DIRECTOR OF TWO AWARD-WINNING ANIMATED SHORTS.